D1331121

THE POLITICS O

KEY TEXT
REFERENCE

MANCHESTER MEDIEVAL STUDIES

SERIES EDITOR Dr S. H. Rigby

SERIES ADVISORS Professor J. H. Denton
Professor R. B. Dobson Professor L. K. Little

The study of medieval Europe is being transformed as old orthodoxies are challenged, new methods embraced and fresh fields of inquiry opened up. The adoption of inter-disciplinary perspectives and the challenge of economic, social and cultural theory are forcing medievalists to ask new questions and to see familiar topics in a fresh light.

The aim of this series is to combine the scholarship traditionally associated with medieval studies with an awareness of more recent issues and approaches in a form accessible to the non-specialist reader.

ALREADY PUBLISHED IN THE SERIES

The commercialisation of English society, 1000–1500
R. H. Britnell

Picturing women in late Medieval and Renaissance art
Christa Grössinger

Law in context   Anthony Musson

Chaucer in context   S. H. Rigby

MANCHESTER MEDIEVAL STUDIES

THE POLITICS
OF CARNIVAL
FESTIVE MISRULE
IN MEDIEVAL ENGLAND

Chris Humphrey

Manchester University Press
Manchester and New York

distributed exclusively in the USA by Palgrave

The right of Chris Humphrey to be identified as the author of this work has been asserted
by him in accorance with the Copyright, Designs and Patents Act 1988

Published by Manchester University Press
Oxford Road, Manchester M13 9NR, UK
and Room 400, 175 Fifth Avenue, New York, NY 10010, USA
http://www.manchesteruniversitypress.co.uk

Distributed exclusively in the USA
by Palgrave, 175 Fifth Avenue, New York, NY 10010, USA

Distributed exclusively in Canada
by UBC Press, University of British Columbia, 2029 West Mall,
Vancouver, BC, Canada V6T 1Z2

British Library Cataloguing-in-Publication Data
A catalogue record for this book is available from the British Library

Library of Congress Cataloging-in-Publication Data applied for

ISBN 0 7190 5602 0 *hardback*
ISBN 0 7190 5603 9 *paperback*

First published 2001

08   07   06   05   04   03   02   01   10   9   8   7   6   5   4   3   2   1

Typeset in Monotype Bulmer
by Koinonia, Manchester
Printed in Great Britain
by Bell and Bain Ltd, Glasgow

For my parents

The problem of *carnival* (in the sense of the sum total of all diverse festivities, rituals and forms of a carnival type) – its essence, its deep roots in the primordial order and the primordial thinking of man, its development under conditions of class society, its extraordinary life force and its undying fascination – is one of the most complex and most interesting problems in the history of culture. We cannot, of course, do justice to it here.

Mikhail Bakhtin, *Problems of Dostoevsky's Poetics*

CONTENTS

PREFACE

As the great Russian scholar Mikhail Bakhtin has noted, the origins and development of carnival are one of the most complex and most interesting problems in the history of culture, and scholarly interest in the subject has continued to grow during the 1980s and 1990s. With carnival forms now being discussed across a range of disciplines, from criminology to cultural studies, carnival is the touchstone for all kinds of hot topics like subversion, transgression and popular resistance to authority. One fascinating aspect of this booming literature is its continual recourse to the question of carnival's medieval origins, as a way of deciding whether carnival and popular culture are capable of acting as a force for social change, or whether they merely represent a 'safety-valve', a licensed and ultimately contained explosion of popular energies. Bakhtin's exuberant picture of medieval and Renaissance carnival life has proved inconclusive in resolving what we might call the 'subversion or containment' question, although if we turn for clarification to studies of medieval festal culture over the past two decades, the overwhelming sense there is of carnival and comparable festivities working in the service of the status quo. Carnival, marching watches, hocking, festive drama, boy-bishops, even morris dancing - all of these customs and practices have been seen as ways of dissipating the radical or socially transformative energies of medieval men, women and children.

The present book is written with the sense that a sustained examination of the question of the function of carnival and its associated forms in the Middle Ages would be of benefit to students and scholars in a number of disciplines. There are two areas in particular which deserve further attention. First, we urgently need a more satisfactory way of talking about the functions of carnival and comparable practices than the 'subversion or containment' binary permits. This is of course by no means an original argument, as the limitations of the safety-valve view have been pointed out by historians and social theorists for some time now. That said, these arguments have not yet been fully appreciated in some areas of study, particularly in relation to the medieval evidence, where the safety-valve view of festivity still appears to hold sway. A second area is to think more critically about how we deduce meanings from the evidence, as all too often the functions and meaning of customs are derived by comparison with abstract models, rather than by means of studies which explore and contextualise their social dimension. With these two needs in mind therefore, this book sets out a more constructive framework for characterising and approaching the medieval evidence, and it consolidates this method by showing the kinds of contextualised and arguably more productive readings of the evidence that it can produce.

This book aims to be concise, specific and above all helpful, and so it does not try to survey all the possible material, either in the sources or in terms of scholarly comment. So while the European context is mentioned where relevant, the main focus is on the English evidence, almost exclusively urban in its derivation, and on the whole from the fifteenth century. Also, Bakhtin's work or influence in this field is not covered in anything like the depth which it merits, since that would occupy a book in itself. Discussions of secondary sources in each section are clearly not exhaustive, and instead references to further reading are given where appropriate. All in all, the object has been to give sufficient references to carry the force of the arguments forward, while avoiding burdening the reader with too much detail.

In terms of the wider reading which informs this study, there are a number of works which deserve a brief mention here. Stallybrass and White's classic study of cultural boundaries and their transgression from the seventeenth century onwards is essential and compulsive reading, and to some extent my own research interests have sought to supply the missing medieval dimension to their otherwise exemplary account of *The Politics and Poetics of Transgression*. Anyone working on the topic of calendar customs and the ritual year will be indebted as I have been to the work of two historians, Ronald Hutton and Charles Phythian-Adams. Hutton's synthesis of the medieval evidence in *The Rise and Fall of Merry England* has informed my general understanding of festive customs in this period, whilst Phythian-Adams's discussion of methodologies in *Local History and Folklore* has proved invaluable for my sense of what a new framework for approaching misrule should include. James Scott's study of the politics of subordinate groups, *Domination and the Arts of Resistance*, explores in fascinating depth many of the issues which I am only able to touch upon in the present volume, and I hope that my own use of Scott's work will bring it the wider appreciation in the arts and humanities which it clearly deserves. Finally, despite its limitations as a historical account, Mikhail Bakhtin's remarkable consideration of medieval and Renaissance festal culture in *Rabelais and his World* has been a continual reminder of what is at stake in the politics of carnival.

A number of people and institutions deserve thanks for their help in bringing this project to fruition. I am grateful to the British Academy for funding the doctoral and postdoctoral work on which this book is based. I would like to thank the staff at the Norwich, Bristol, Coventry and York record offices and archives for all their assistance during my research. The staff at Manchester University Press and the readers who generously commented on the drafts have made the publication process a smooth and enjoyable one. The Centre for Medieval Studies at the University of York is an exciting and stimulating place to work, and I would like to thank all the students and staff who have discussed ideas and sources with me in the course of this project. I am grateful to Nick Havely and Charles Phythian-Adams for their advice and opinion when it really mattered, and to Max Harris and Tim Reuter, who drew my attention to the importance of James Scott's work. John Arnold has been a close friend for many years and his unflagging enthusiasm for discussing both theory and evidence with me deserves special thanks. I owe a particular debt to John McGavin, Jeremy Goldberg and Felicity Riddy, who supervised my work at various stages and who have always been a constant source of help, guidance and inspiration to me. Finally, I will always be grateful to Rachel, Isobel, my parents and the rest of my family and friends for all the love and support that they have so generously given.

NOTE ON THE TEXT AND ABBREVIATIONS

Thorns and yoghs have been replaced as appropriate, and capitalisation and punctuation have been modified in the quotations from records that I have transcribed myself. The spelling of names has been left in the original where that person appears only once or twice; the names of individuals who are cited more often have been standardised in line with modern usage. All medieval dates are given in New Style.

A condensed version of material from chapters 1 and 2 has appeared in print as 'The world upside down in theory and as practice: a new approach to the study of medieval misrule', *Medieval English Theatre* 21 (1999), 5–20. An earlier version of chapter 3 appeared in print as '"To make a new king": seasonal drama and local politics in Norwich, 1443', *Medieval English Theatre* 17 (1995), 29–41. A shorter version of chapter 4 appeared in print as 'Festive drama and community politics in late medieval Coventry, in *Drama and Community: People and Plays in Medieval Europe*, ed. A. Hindley, Medieval Texts and Cultures of Northern Europe 1, Turnhout, 1999, pp. 217–30. I am grateful for permission from Brepols publishers to reproduce this material.

The few abbreviations which have been used are listed below:

CRO	Coventry Record Office
EETS	Early English Text Society
MED	*Middle English Dictionary*
NRO	Norwich Record Office
OED	*Oxford English Dictionary*
OS	Original Series
REED	Records of Early English Drama
YCA	York City Archives

The politics of carnival

G iven that the principal characteristic of carnival-style festivities is a noisy interruption of everyday public life, it is perhaps not surprising that there should be numerous mentions of them in the historical record. Whether it be the fulminations of medieval bishops, the vibrant world conjured by writers like Goethe and Rabelais, or the close observations of modern folklorists, a range of records and texts capture the diversity and vitality of this remarkable genre of popular festive culture. From the perspective of the academic study of the social and cultural life of the past, these descriptive records are an invaluable source of information for illustrating the life and culture of particular places and periods. Not surprisingly, the studies which have drawn upon this evidence make for fascinating reading: who could fail to be enthralled by Le Roy Ladurie's account of the epic festive battles at Romans in the 1570s, or by Bakhtin's enthusiastic engagement with the literary art of Rabelais?

That said, it is also the case that many accounts of carnival move rather quickly into complex discussions of its meanings, so that the energy and vitality of the subject are drowned in a sea of critical terms. All the talk of 'safety-valves' and 'subversion', and the variety of opinions and arguments on offer can be off-putting, making it difficult to get a sense of the general picture. The preoccupation with abstract theories and difficult jargon has come about because researchers have been interested in more than just the customs themselves: there is also the question

1

of how festival occasions might reflect wider social concerns such as class or gender divisions. In plain terms this means thinking about how rivalries or antagonisms between different groups, such as those separated by rank or wealth, are exacerbated or at least made more prominent during moments of seasonal change like Lent, New Year and midsummer. This concern with what we can call 'the politics of carnival' has led to all kinds of speculation about the meaning of particular calendar customs, ranging from the idea that they represent a kind of opposition to the established order of society, through to the notion that by overstepping certain boundaries, their participants are merely reaffirming them in the long run (the safety-valve view).[1] On the whole what is happening here is that carnival is being seen as more than just a seasonal entertainment or celebration - it is seen as the voice of an oppressed majority, or as a means through which political control over that majority is cunningly exercised. It is fair to say that it is not always clear how such conclusions are deduced from the evidence; fairly complex arguments or models from other disciplines such as anthropology or social science are often introduced. Also, given that there are these competing characterisations of carnival's meaning, there is the deeper logical issue of which of them might be the more correct or persuasive.

These observations, commonly raised in relation to the study of this kind of material, can be re-formulated as a series of questions that readers and researchers in this area might ask: what are the main approaches? Which of these views of carnival's social role is the more valid? What kind of approach can best make sense of any new evidence which we encounter? What does a successful analysis which uses this approach look like? The aim of this book is to provide some considered answers to these questions for students of literature, drama, history and popular culture, for whom the politics of carnival are a crucial issue in the history of festivity and its representation. As such, it offers a guide to approaches rather than a full consideration of all of the practices themselves. Given carnival's vast geographical and chronological occurrence, the field of study is potentially huge, and so the present study only covers these issues for the festive culture of England and particularly its towns in the fifteenth century, both in terms of what has been written by scholars about it, and by exploring in close detail the actual historical evidence from the period. Using these materials, the different kinds of approaches can be explained and their relative merits weighed up, the most effective method for analysis established, and this method can be seen to work by applying it to some actual historical examples. Overall, it will be possible to resolve many of the issues which have complicated this area of study, enabling the investigation of these festive forms to move forward in a more constructive way.

In narrowing the focus to the evidence from medieval England however, some care is needed as regards the terms of reference that are used. The term 'carnival' is often used as a catch-all term to describe any festival occasion that pushes at the boundaries of what is considered to be safe, normal and acceptable, in order to surprise, exhilarate and shock audiences and performers alike. That said, it is not really a suitable term for medieval England, as there is not the evidence for Shrovetide plays and celebrations on anything like the scale that is found on the continent.[2] In the light of this difference, this book will use the term 'misrule' rather than carnival in the medieval English context, since the former is a contemporary word which neatly captures the sense of a festive practice which startles or upsets everyday expectations, without implying that it was associated with the Lenten season.[3] In any case 'misrule' has been used to describe a wider set of festive practices for many years now.[4] In turn, where the term 'carnival' is used, this will be in a self-conscious way, to refer to a particular understanding and vision of the past found in the scholarly literature. The capitalised version of the word will then be reserved for those festivities which were and continue to be associated with Shrovetide proper. The adjective 'carnivalesque' is another general term which can be used to describe art or activities which convey a sense of copiousness, abundance or transgression, from ancient times through to the present day.

Table 1 *Festive misrule in medieval England*

Feast and season names (ecclesiastical name in brackets)	Calendar date(s)	Participants and examples
Feast of the boy-bishop (Feasts of St Nicholas and the Holy Innocents)	6 and 28 December	Election of a chorister or other junior to a higher rank in cathedrals and parish churches
Christmas (Feast of St Thomas to Epiphany).	21 December to 6 January	Lords and abbots of misrule Mumming
Feast of Fools, New Year's Day (Feast of the Circumcision).	1 January	Lesser clergy Liturgical inversion and parody
Shrove Tuesday Shrovetide	Associated with the movable feast of Easter	'Gladman's riding', Norwich, 1443
Hock Monday and Hock Tuesday, Hocktide	Second or third Monday and Tuesday after Easter Sunday[a]	Hocking; on the alternate days of Hocktide, groups of men and women would threaten to bind the opposite sex with ropes and charge money for their release
May Day (Sts Philip and Jacob)	1 May	Early rising on May Day to gather vegetation for decoration and to erect maypoles
Midsummer (Nativity of St John Baptist and Feast of Sts Peter and Paul)	24 and 29 June	Election of summer lords and ladies Summer games and bonfires

[a]The date of Hocktide is commonly given by modern scholars as the second Monday and Tuesday after Easter Sunday. However, many antiquarians give the date as the third Monday and Tuesday after Easter Sunday, a formula which is corroborated by the few examples of medieval dating evidence that I have been able to trace (Humphrey, 'Dynamics of urban festal culture', Appendix).

Source: Harper, *Forms and Orders of Western Liturgy* and Hutton, *Stations of the Sun.*

The customs which may be considered under the heading of misrule in medieval England are given in Table 1. As this table shows, these customs took place at well-defined times of the year, as part of an annual calendar cycle of saint's days, religious feasts and popular observances. While they all share a common feature in that they turn upside-down or break with established rules or norms in some way, otherwise they were clearly quite diverse in terms of where they took place, or who was involved in them. This diversity again raises problems in relation to terminology, since none of the usual generic terms such as drama, ritual, ceremony or play really hold for all examples of misrule. Therefore it makes sense to talk about misrule as 'performance', since as the performance theorist Richard Schechner suggests, this is an inclusive term which enables us to recognise a range of sites, styles and meanings.[5] A further advantage of this term is that it reminds us that what gets recorded in historical documents is often just one part of a much larger and more time-consuming effort: again, to cite Schechner, '[g]enerally, scholars have paid attention to the show, not to the whole seven-part sequence of training, workshops, rehearsals, warm-ups, performance, cool-down, and aftermath'.[6]

The English evidence for misrule offers a sound basis for making informed judgements about the larger of question of the politics of carnival. There are plenty of records surviving which can help to show the role (if any) which misrule played in local politics and in the negotiation of social relationships in late medieval England. The first part of this book considers the approaches which have been taken to this evidence in the 1980s and 1990s. Some of these approaches are descriptive, while others which go further and argue for particular views of its function. There are two things that can be done here. First, a closer look at this literature will provide a guide to it, helping to make sense of the different approaches that exist. At this point it is worth noting that the overwhelming argument made about misrule is the one which says that these customs operated as a socially conservative force in late medieval society. The idea is that misrule acts as a 'safety-valve': the metaphor of a controlled release of pent-up steam is used to suggest that by temporarily inverting norms, it enabled the frustrations of socially subordinate groups to be dissipated, and thereby helped to maintain the status quo. Second, this literature can also be thought about in a more critical way, in order to work out the most persuasive means of approaching and analysing the evidence.

So this book begins by explaining the different views which can be found in the secondary literature on medieval misrule and historical views of carnival. Although there are various schools of thought which have approached the subject of misrule in different ways, all of these areas have to some extent become deadlocked around the question of what misrule was, and how it worked. My suggestion therefore is that we need an approach which can take account of the range of views expressed, rather than attempting to privilege just one. In the process it can be shown that while the 'safety-valve' model of misrule addresses some very important themes regarding the role of misrule, this model is none the less inadequate both as a metaphor and as a tool for the analysis of these themes. Furthermore, the view that medieval misrule constituted an entirely oppositional or radical culture, a view which is often extrapolated from the work of Mikhail Bakhtin, is also at odds with the historical evidence. Chapter 1 concludes by suggesting that in order to appreciate fully the dynamics of misrule in these areas, it is necessary to devise a new approach which takes these criticisms into account.

This leads us into chapter 2, where a more appropriate approach to the evidence for medieval misrule is outlined. The main point here is that we take into account the variety of ways that misrule might work. This chapter also considers the three areas that an improved understanding of misrule needs to address, which are a more critical approach to the evidence and what can be deduced from it, a better appreciation of the diversity of possible functions that misrule was able to have, and a closer reading of the particular context in which the performance took place.

Having formulated the best approach, the remainder of the book then proceeds to show how this approach can be brought to bear on the sources for medieval misrule, in order to better understand how particular customs were implicated in the politics and social structure of late medieval society. This is accomplished in two chapters, each of which explores a particular calendar custom from a different English town. By approaching them as dynamic and structuring events in the larger cultural life of the town, a fuller reading of the meaning of these performances can be given. These chapters also help to support the new characterisation of misrule that is discussed in chapter 2. So the discussion of Gladman's riding at Norwich in 1443 in chapter 3 underlines the need to appreciate the potential mobility of festive drama and consider the reasons why it might take place outside of its usual calendar occurrence, while chapter 4 considers how the cutting down of vegetation formed part of a wider oppositional campaign in late medieval Coventry, showing the importance of exploring how calendar customs might be bound up with particular kinds of political strategies. When taken together, these studies by no means provide an overarching synthesis of all the evidence for misrule in the period, but they do illustrate the kinds of analyses that are necessary for developing a more comprehensive understanding of the social dynamics of medieval festive drama.

It is helpful to mention in brief the records which underpin the methodological approach and the case studies which are set out in this book. In an earlier study I looked at the dynamics of misrule in four English towns, Bristol, Coventry, Norwich and York from the late fourteenth century to the early sixteenth century. These towns were chosen for the accessibility and the depth of their primary source material.[7] The present book makes use of material from two of those towns, Norwich and Coventry, for the case study chapters. For Coventry the town's first Leet Book provides an extremely full account of civic affairs from 1420 onwards, while Norwich has a good range of documentary sources including the Liber Albus.[8] Also useful are urban churchwardens' accounts, the records of income and expenditure that were kept by the wardens of parish churches, and which often contain more detailed information about the activities upon which money was spent.[9] Inevitably, the decision to concentrate upon these reasonably comparable sources means that the view of misrule given here is predominantly an urban one, and it is beyond the scope of this volume to address questions about the extent to which the festal culture of rural and urban areas differed, or whether the situation in the large cities was markedly different from that in smaller towns. None the less, the general principles that we should not essentialise misrule, and that our understanding of its social dimensions needs to be based upon a closer analysis where possible, still apply to these contexts.

Although this book is primarily concerned with medieval misrule, the sources and issues which are discussed are also relevant for the wider debates in the humanities and social sciences which centre around questions of resistance, agency and transgression in popular culture. Medievalists concerned about the marginality of their discipline need only look to recent issues of periodicals in cultural studies and related fields, where the idea of medieval carnival is clearly flourishing. Here Mikhail Bakhtin's descriptions of carnival have been used as a yardstick against which to compare all kinds of more recent practices, in an attempt to determine whether their social impetus works to transform the current state of society.[10] Other studies in the social sciences such as James Scott's book on *Domination and the Arts of Resistance* have also addressed the question of how the political strategies of subordinate groups might be better understood, and carnival has been one of the practices that has been considered. So in putting forward an argument about the dynamics of medieval festal culture which is firmly grounded in the historical evidence from fifteenth-century England, this book also makes an original contribution to a range of areas of enquiry outside of medieval studies. For example, in relation to the issue of whether popular culture is able to effect social change, it is shown that misrule could indeed work to this end in the medieval period, although this is seen as a consequence of wider contextual factors, rather than because of any inherent oppositional quality to misrule. In addition, by demonstrating the distance between the idea of medieval carnival circulating in cultural studies and the view which can be derived from historical sources, the limitations of the use of the idea of carnival as a privileged decoder of cultural meanings are revealed. The implication in both cases is that in seeking to understand the dynamics of popular culture, a crucial task must be to explore the immediate context in which particular practices take place: the utility of historical comparisons is a modest one and certainly not a starting point where the cultural meanings of a practice are concerned. The new methodology and critical terms outlined in this book consequently provide a starting point for a more general contextual analysis of popular culture.

Notes

1 See my extended discussion of this literature in chapter 1.

2 For a discussion of the differences between England and the continent see Davidson, 'Carnival, Lent and drama', pp. 123-4 and Johnston, 'The continental connection', p. 21.

3 *MED misreule* n. (1) [a], [b] and (2) [a], [b] are on the whole pejorative, but it is clear that contemporaries also used this word in a non-pejorative way, for example as a title for the person who presided over a series of festivities. See the numerous examples of abbots and lords of misrule collected in Lancashire, *Dramatic Texts and Records of Britain*.

4 See for example Davis, 'The reasons of misrule' and Hutton, *Stations of the Sun*.

5 Schechner, *Performance Theory*, p. xiii.

6 Schechner, *Between Theater and Anthropology*, p. 16. While I am not suggesting that all examples of misrule were necessarily rehearsed, thinking about misrule in this way can help us to develop a more sophisticated view of how performances unfolded over time.

7 Humphrey, 'Dynamics of urban festal culture'.

8 For edited editions of this material see *The Coventry Leet Book*, ed. M. D. Harris, 2 vols, EETS OS 134, 135, 138 and 146 (1907-13) and *The Records of the City of Norwich*, ed. W. Hudson and J. C. Tingey, 2 vols, Norwich and London, 1906-10.

9 See the list of churchwardens' accounts in Hutton, *Rise and Fall of Merry England*, pp. 263-93.

10 See for example Gregson and Crewe, 'The bargain, the knowledge, and the spectacle' and Kohl, 'Looking through a glass onion'. For a discussion of the limitations of these kinds of comparisons see Humphrey, 'Bakhtin and popular culture'.

Social protest or safety-valve?
Critical approaches to festive misrule

Introduction

Interest in the festive culture of fifteenth- and sixteenth-century England goes right back to the period itself, when the London citizen John Stow sought to record the principal shows and festive customs of his city that were ongoing, or were within his living memory. A later writer like Joseph Strutt (1801) wanted to formulate a view of the national character of the English based upon a historical study of their sports and pastimes: he was sorely disappointed by much of what he found. As with all enquiries into the past, people's pre-occupations shift and change, so that what was once a burning issue can seem with hindsight to be obscure or difficult to reconcile with the current interests and ideas. The predominant interests in medieval misrule in 1980s and 1990s have come from three main directions: urban history and the culture of medieval towns; medieval drama and festive life; and the wider history of drama and popular culture. In all of these fields, there has been a concern to collect evidence together, in order to reconstruct the main customs and their characteristics. In addition, a recurrent theme has been to ask of misrule, what was its wider social role and meaning? As already mentioned, on the whole the trend has been to see misrule as a 'safety-valve': the idea is that if people are able to break the rules on one day of the year, they are thereby able to vent their anxieties and frustrations, and so will be more likely to behave themselves for the rest of the year. Festive occasions on which the boundaries of everyday behaviour were overstepped can therefore be seen, ironically, as a means through which unequal relations of power and opportunity – patriarchy, lordship, oligarchy – were perpetuated in the cultures where misrule occurs.

This view of misrule has been a popular one, since it appears to reconcile the apparently rebellious aspect of these customs with a lack of evidence to suggest that this topsy-turvy world ever became an actual reality. It also enjoys a wide currency in many other disciplines, so much so that to quote one writer on the subject, '[i]f issues of interpretation like this were resolved on the basis of a majority vote of scholars who had looked at the matter, the safety-valve theory would almost surely prevail'.[1] That said, there are other views of misrule too, which reach rather different conclusions about what meanings it had for performers and audiences. The present chapter considers the range of ways that researchers working on the festal culture of medieval England have thought about misrule. The most influential studies and conclusions in each of the three areas identified earlier will be covered.

A common thread running through this chapter will be that although there is a large secondary literature on festive misrule and on carnival more generally, it is actually quite difficult to find answers to two of the most commonly-asked questions. These are: which of the views of misrule and its social role is the most valid; and what kind of approach can best make sense of the evidence and explain the meaning of particular examples of festivity? Questions of this sort arise when students or researchers need to comment upon the nature of misrule, or when they are faced with some evidence of which they want to make sense. In the first case, what is being sought is a definition of misrule, a clear statement of the kind of cultural activity that it is. The problem is that there are many examples of such definitions in circulation, and that as they tend to contradict one another, it can be difficult to judge which of them is the most valid. A definition that is properly explained and backed up with evidence would therefore be very helpful. In the course of this chapter the extent to which particular approaches to medieval misrule do adequately define misrule will be considered.

As regards the second question posed above, something else that is often looked for in the secondary literature is a set of guidelines on how to interpret the evidence for particular customs. Although we may want to know more about intriguing activities that we read about, and what such events meant to those who took part, it can be often be difficult to see how to investigate them further, since books and articles about misrule tend to present conclusions rather than methods for research. Not only that, but the safety-valve theory has no need for such tools, since it already claims to know how all such occasions worked: they were merely an outlet for resentment and frustration. The second aim of this chapter is therefore to review how useful the existing approaches really are in this practical respect.

One very important point that will emerge in the course of this chapter is that generalisations about the role of misrule tend to hinder rather than help our interpretation of it. Therefore, the more that we can see performances of misrule as meaningful in their own right, rather than just having the same effects over and over again as predicted by an abstract model, the more sensitive we can be to the subtleties and intricacies of the evidence that we study. This approach, which also stands as a new agenda for the future study of misrule and carnival forms, will be considered in more detail in chapter 2. Constraints of space mean that this survey of relevant sources must be selective, and so not all works or areas of study which have touched on this theme are covered. In particular important studies of the early modern period in Europe such as those by Burke, Davis and Le Roy Ladurie are not discussed in any depth, although reference is made to them where pertinent.[2] Neither has it been possible to consider the many literary studies which draw upon the notion of carnival and the carnivalesque.[3]

Approaches to festive misrule in medieval English towns

In many ways the cities and towns of late medieval Europe appear as places of extremes: contemporaries praised their stunning architecture and virtuous citizens as well as condemning their terrible odours and corrupting lifestyle, while later research has shown the decisive role which cities played in the formation of many aspects of modern culture. In fact a closer look shows that medieval towns were less a marriage of opposites and more a loose alliance of diverse social groups (merchants, artisans, clergy, the poor) and their institutions (guilds, councils, courts, churches) in a compact, fortified space. It is not surprising therefore that many different forms of festive and popular life flourished in the medieval town, each reflecting the needs and aspirations of particular groups and the influence of local traditions. In England, this could involve large-scale public events such as plays dramatising the events from the creation of the world until the Last Judgement (mystery plays), celebrations for the entry of a monarch into the city (royal entries), through to smaller-scale events such as guild feasts, street processions and the usual suspects like football, archery and tennis.

The festive culture of towns has received a considerable amount of attention from scholars, either as part of a more general discussion of urban life, or in the consideration of particular genres of drama or festivity. The source materials used for these studies have been the records of civic business kept by the towns themselves in the Middles Ages, such as minutes from council meetings and financial records, and the centralised records of the monarch and the government, in which town affairs are often mentioned. In the discussions of urban life which can be derived from these sources misrule has not featured as a discrete area of inquiry in itself, but rather it has been considered in discussions of the wider range of ceremonial occasions which took place in towns. In this respect the pioneering work of Charles Phythian-Adams and Mervyn James on urban ritual and ceremony has established an influential model which much later work has followed. The trend has been for a dual model, where both more formal ceremony and less institutionalised practices like misrule are perceived to work together as a means of regulating urban life.

Such a case was outlined in Phythian-Adams's ground-breaking essay on 'Ceremony and the citizen: the communal year at Coventry 1450–1550', which was first published in 1972 in a collection of essays on urban history. Its originality, range of sources and depth of analysis have ensured that it has remained a key text; it has recently been reprinted in an urban history reader.[4] As well as offering an extremely full account of the civic year in Coventry in the later Middle Ages, covering ceremonies of oath-taking, dinners, processions, drinkings, dancing, evergreen-decking and plays, Phythian-Adams also considers the social function of the rituals which are described. For example, when discussing those 'periodic relaxations of the social order' that took place on festival occasions in Coventry, such as the Hock Tuesday play or the May Day celebrations, he suggests that '[i]f such customs deliberately distorted certain aspects of the social order, there was no question of altering the whole: in disfiguring the structure temporarily, the participants were in fact accepting the *status quo* in the long run'. Phythian-Adams goes on to conclude:

> And it was perhaps this emphasis on preserving and enhancing the wholeness of the social order which most distinguished the ceremonies of this late medieval urban community. In a close-knit structure composed of overlapping groups or groupings, where a change of status in one sphere so often could affect standing in another, ceremony performed a crucial clarifying role. It was a societal mechanism ensuring continuity within the structure, promoting cohesion and controlling some of its inherent conflicts, which was not only valued as contributing to the 'worship' of the city, but also enjoyed by contemporaries. Even in times of crisis the plays were performed and the watches marched.[5]

The interpretation is that because misrule only broke with certain boundaries and norms, it did not actually attempt to threaten the social order itself. This point of view was put forward in a more general way in Phythian-Adams's excellent guide to the study of social customs in his book *Local History and Folklore*.[6]

The other important and influential study, which appeared in 1983, was Mervyn James's essay on the social function of the plays and processions which took place on or around Corpus Christi day in the late medieval town. Noting that previous writers on the Corpus Christi cult possessed only a very general idea of the social context to the celebrations which accompanied the feast in towns, James sets out his aims as follows:

> Briefly, I propose to argue that the theme of Corpus Christi is society seen in terms of body; and that the concept of body provided urban societies with a mythology and ritual in terms of which the opposites of social wholeness and social differentiation could be both affirmed, and also brought into a creative tension, one with the other. The final intention of the cult was, then, to express the social bond and to contribute to social integration.[7]

In James's view the underlining of social difference within a wider frame of shared values was accomplished on the festive occasion. This worked since on the one hand the hierarchical nature of the Corpus Christi procession, where the guilds of a town processed through the streets in order of their rank or worth, was able to impart an ordered structure to the sense of 'undifferentiated togetherness' which the occasion created. As a complement to this, the Corpus Christi plays that were mounted by guilds on individual wagons cycles, and which could therefore reflect the changing status and wealth of that guild, 'provided a mechanism ... by which the tensions implicit in the diachronic rise and fall of occupational communities could be confronted and worked out.'[8]

The balancing of difference within wholeness: it is this idea which has made the work of Phythian-Adams and James so influential on both the general and the more specific studies of the function of ceremony in the late medieval town. For example, Peter Womack has referred to them together as two 'classic studies' in his discussion of medieval urban Corpus Christi plays and processions.[9] That said, other scholars have been less convinced about the success of the unifying effects of formal ceremonial and play-performance. In a review of studies of English religious fraternities Sheila Lindenbaum has distinguished between those accounts which have perceived fraternities as working to sustain communal bonds and those which stress their exclusiveness and dedication to class interests.[10] Lindenbaum suggests that pursuing the latter line of enquiry 'encourages us to question some well-established notions about the drama, specifically the idea that except for entertainment at court and in the noble households, medieval drama and ceremonial was largely a collective enterprise – a communal ritual in which all took part and which gave diverse groups within the community a sense of unity and shared identity'. Lindenbaum suggests that this view is 'best represented' by Phythian-Adams's article on 'Ceremony and the citizen' and James's article on 'Ritual, drama and social body', and goes on to make several points in respect of the latter's views of how Corpus Christi processions and guild pageants worked to create and express wholeness.[11] One is that the idea of the body as a means by which diverse members might be unified into a whole should not be interpreted literally, as an indication of actual power relations, because guild membership was exclusive; therefore, not everyone was able to participate in the 'social body' that is held to have been created through the procession and play cycle either. Another point is that spectators need not have felt unity with those in the procession as it passed through the streets, and indeed its exclusivity may have worked against any such identification.[12] Other studies raising similar kinds of objections may be cited.[13]

Part of the reason for disagreement here is the definition of community which is at stake – does it include everyone in the town, or is it confined to a majority, or even a minority? It is often overlooked that Phythian-Adams offers a fairly restricted definition of community at the beginning of his essay, as one which excludes approximately 20 per cent of male householders and all single females under forty.[14] In relation to the social role of ceremony and celebration, the issue is that while those on the 'inside' of these events may have felt their communal ties strengthened by participating, those on the 'outside' may well have not. Clearly, the attitude which one takes to the views and feelings of those less directly involved in festive events, and where the line is drawn between inside and out, is crucial when it comes to interpreting the meaning of such occasions. In fact misrule is often seen to provide some form of compensation for those groups who tended to be excluded from or played a less visible role in formal civic occasions, such as younger adults or women. The idea is that misrule could act as an outlet for the expression of resentment about one's marginalised status, but with the consequence that these frustrations had no lasting effects, due to the temporary nature of the occasion. Misrule is therefore seen as being complicit with authority, in the very act of defying that authority.

For example, Barbara Hanawalt has discussed how the 'riot and misrule' associated with the youth of medieval London could be channelled on festival occasions. Observing that '[m]uch of the frustration that led to riot centred on deprivation of adult status rather than a desire to prolong or glorify youth', Hanawalt goes on to argue that:

> London tried to accommodate the need for a youthful release by making such holidays as St. John's Eve (Midsummer Eve) a time for general celebration, feasting, and bonfires, as well as the evening during which the mayor, the aldermen, and the respectable men of the ward paraded in the principal streets carrying torches. This was the famous Midsummer Watch. At Christmas as well, London permitted all sorts of sporting events.

Hanawalt then balances this statement with the observation that 'the city ordinances indicate a fear that the festivities might turn to riot', giving examples of the prohibition of masking and the early closure of taverns on holidays.[15] Such a view of misrule as a release of potentially destructive energies has also been used in a comparative way. For example, in a discussion of representations of the city in medieval manuscripts Michael Camille makes a comparison between his view of the functions of both 'carnival' and marginal art in relation to 'the official order':

> Often licensed by the civic authorities, all the inversion, cross-dressing, riotous drinking and parodic performance at carnival time was a carefully controlled valve for letting off steam. In this sense, carnival seems similar to what we have seen going on in the manuscript margins, since in both carnival and marginal art what looks at first like unfettered freedom of expression often served to legitimate the status quo, chastising the weaker groups in the social order, such as women and ethnic and social minorities. We have to face up to carnival's complicity with the official order, played out in the supposed subversion of it.[16]

These two examples demonstrate the popularity of the view that occasions of misrule worked in the interests of the status quo in the medieval period.

Not all scholars have taken such a conservative line however. Although concerned with the country rather than the town, Steven Justice considers the oppositional nature of midsummer bonfires in relation to the English Rising of 1381. Justice makes reference to Phythian-Adams's suggestion that the theft of vegetation on some calendar festivals was tolerated in this period: '[a]t certain times of the year, it would seem, the great landholders had to accept that the laws of property, which normally sustained their positions, might be briefly ignored by right of custom.'[17] Justice goes on to note that '[r]ecent discussion of popular ceremonies has tended to decide that their contained, seasonal character necessarily undermined any oppositional stance', citing Bakhtin and discussions of his work.[18] Justice's alternative line of reasoning is to ask 'whether the festivities might serve, and the opposition therefore be subordinate to, some other purpose internal to the community, defined independently of (not in response to, and not therefore in the terms of) the power that rules it'. He argues that while the gathering of wood for midsummer bonfires encroached on the lord's forest, this encroachment was not an end in itself; rather, it was instrumental to the needs of the village at the crucial time of harvest. 'The common grudge against lordship relieved internal pressures by scapegoating (not all scapegoating is unjust; sometimes it just acknowledges fact) and presumably celebrated the self-sufficiency of the community, its ability to resolve its differences and manage its affairs independent of the lord.'[19] Other studies which raise similar points may also be mentioned.[20]

It should be clear from this discussion that there are a range of views about how festival occasions worked. The argument that they functioned as a conservative and cohesive force in medieval towns is well established with regard to both formal civic occasions and to misrule, but this view has also been criticised on several fronts. On the whole then, arguments about misrule have been put in rather exclusive terms; either misrule works like a safety-valve, and the status quo is restored after a period of temporary inversion, or it is seen as the expression of class antagonism or gender politics. There is not much scope for views in between. Different points of view like these are not really a problem if we are just surveying the various approaches in order to see the current state of the literature, as has been done so far. However, difficulties do begin to arise when the answers to more specific questions are sought. For example, there is an early sixteenth-century English–French dictionary which includes the phrase 'Lette us go mumme to nyght in womens apparayle', whose meaning is something like 'let us go mumming tonight, calling on houses and collecting money while disguised as women'. Assuming that this might be the kind of thing that two butcher's apprentices from Newcastle could have plotted over a pint of ale at Christmas (since mumming by apprentices was prohibited in that town in 1554), how should this kind of behaviour be interpreted?[21] Do we follow the line suggested for medieval London, and see this custom as another means for controlling social tensions within an urban community? If so, what kinds of tensions does your average butcher's apprentice from Newcastle experience, and how might this control them?

One solution is just to go with what seems the more persuasive interpretation: either we take the view that medieval misrule is on the whole a form of social control, or a form of social opposition, depending upon our personal preference and reasoning. This seems to be what many writers on this subject have in fact done: one view or another has been accepted as the 'natural' or 'obvious' way that misrule worked, and the evidence has been interpreted in these terms alone. Reasons for and against particular approaches are not always discussed, and if they are it is usually fairly briefly. For those new to the field, the interpretation of misrule can often seem to be about little more than making this choice, however dissatisfying it might feel: an optimistic reading might prefer to emphasise the dynamic character of the custom, whilst a more pessimistic one may soberly accept its ultimately reactionary nature.

That said, it is possible to take a more imaginative line on the issue of interpretation, which steps back from the limited options discussed so far and takes a more thoughtful to misrule and what it represents. Such an approach starts from the idea that it makes little sense to impose only one kind of inter-pretation on a piece of evidence which we know very little about: surely, more information is needed if any kind of informed conclusion is to be reached. This information might involve looking more closely at the context in which the custom took place, who was involved, how often it took place and so on. Admittedly, this is a more time-consuming process than pigeon-holing misrule as one thing or another, and of course the evidence which is looked for may not always be found. But overall, it seems reasonable to believe that with more details in hand, we can make a better appraisal of the role of the custom than existing modes of interpretation do.

What a review of the current literature in this area doesn't show therefore is that the interpretation of misrule can be about a great deal more that just choosing between the mutually exclusive options of safety-valve or social revolt. Arguably a more successful approach is to keep an open mind about possibilities, and to investigate matters further where the evidence permits. In fact, when this kind of 'contextual' approach is considered, as it will be in more detail in the next chapter, the different points of view very quickly change from being exclusive interpretations, and become possibilities which may or may not be shown up in the evidence. Put another way, whether a particular custom proceeds according to one of these outcomes is something which needs to be ascertained in the specific instance: the meanings and functions of a custom cannot merely be read from its form alone. This is not to imply that what happens in any given case is merely random, or is always going to be different from what went before. Rather, it is to understand that performance outcomes are necessarily the result of a particular set of factors, the balance of which can vary a great deal according to historical and contextual circumstances. Gaining an understanding of these factors is therefore an important part of the way that the meaning of misrule is analysed and interpreted.

To conclude, this review has shown the main approaches that have been taken to the interpretation of the evidence for public ceremony and misrule as it is recorded in the documents of medieval towns. As well as describing these approaches, their usefulness as a means of interpreting new kinds of evidence has been considered. If these views are seen to be generally true about most instances of misrule, then the researcher need do little more than select an interpretation, and use it to make a statement about the custom in question. This arguably makes for dull and predictable scholarship, and is unconvincing if other details which might contradict such interpretations are not explored. A more viable alternative is to reserve our interpretation until a fuller investigation of the custom and its context has been carried out.

Approaches to medieval English drama and calendar customs

Once considered the poor relation of the Renaissance theatre, concerted work on medieval English drama and performance in recent years has had the effect of transforming scholarly and popular perceptions of the genre. New critical editions of the texts of surviving plays have shown the evocative power of their language and imagery, while research into the conditions of performance has underlined how sophisticated and ambitious many productions were. In particular the Records of Early English Drama project, which surveys all references to dramatic activity up to 1642, has furnished a wealth of primary source data which cuts across the traditional periodisation of medieval and early modern. In consequence, the famous dramatic culture of later sixteenth-century England now appears less a new flowering, and more the culmination of a centuries-long tradition of writing and stagecraft, what one commentator has referred to as 'Shakespeare's inheritance'.[22] This emphasis on continuity and the problems with older systems of categorisation has also seen the definition of drama expand, to take in those customs and celebrations associated with important occasions in the calendar year as well as texts written for performance.

That said, analysing the performance of a popular custom is somewhat different to analysing a play text. In the absence of lines of dialogue or a known author, attention has instead focused upon the characteristic features of particular customs, detailing for example the costumes worn, the kinds of people taking part, and the time and place of performances. These sorts of details are found in a variety of sources, including inventories, household account books, eye-witness descriptions and civic records. The motivations behind different performances have also been considered, with a general emphasis on the expression of community values, although this question has been seen by some scholars as an issue which is beyond their brief, or too complex a matter to try to deal with. So, for example, in his introduction to *The Rise and Fall of Merry England* Ronald Hutton notes that he has 'not attempted any discussion of the social function of the different categories of ritual, being satisfied with the broad categories already provided in a book such as Peter Burke's *Popular Culture in Early Modern Europe* (1978)'.[23] Other scholars have felt themselves in a position to make judgements about the social function of calendar customs, and as regards the study of festive misrule, there are two main strands of work that may be considered. There are those studies which comment upon misrule when discussing a wider theme, such as images of reversal in drama or culture more generally. The other relevant studies are those which survey the evidence for particular customs, and offer conclusions about how they work in this context. Each of these strands takes a somewhat different view of the social function of misrule, as a brief consideration of some examples will show.

It would be fair to say that on the whole, those studies which discuss misrule in the context of a larger issue or theme tend to view it as having a range of meanings, compared with those studies that have looked in detail at the evidence for one custom in isolation. This seems to be because these wider analyses take in a range of secondary sources, especially those studies from the early modern period by Yves-Marie Bercé, Natalie Zemon Davis and Emmanuel Le Roy Ladurie, which have offered more open-ended views of how festivity might work.[24] For example, in his consideration of the social meanings of vernacular medieval plays, Anthony Gash has suggested that research into popular festivity is a relevant area for comparison, and he makes the following points about the relationship between drama and festivity:

> The counterpoint of hieratic formality and energetic clowning that pervades medieval drama finds its analogue in the cyclical alternation throughout the year of ceremonies which formalised group relations and idealised social distinctions with ones which symbolically inverted norms.
>
> While English historians such as Phythian-Adams and Keith Thomas believe that the subversive potential of rituals of status-reversal and misrule was generally well controlled, and that their meaning was ultimately conservative, Davis and Le Roy Ladurie

have shown for early modern France how such rituals could also provide occasions and imagery for artisan protests and revolts against tyranny and taxation. In fact, these apparently contrasting findings are not incompatible since the need for regular ritual celebrations of corporate unity are testimony to the conflicts of interest which they sought, and sometimes failed, to reconcile.[24]

The events of the festive calendar are therefore seen as means to explain certain structural features of medieval plays, and in the process misrule is attributed with a variability of function, sometimes conservative and sometimes serving as a vehicle for protest and dissent.

Another study in which the function of misrule is discussed as part of a wider theme is in Sandra Billington's book on *Mock Kings in Medieval Society and Renaissance Drama*. Here the image of the mock king is traced across a range of sources, including medieval drama, festive misrule, and the kinds of titles used by rebels and outlaws. When introducing the secondary literature on the relationship between festivity and rebellion in medieval England and in early modern England and France, Billington observes that '[t]he last fifteen years have seen a fruitful investigation into the symbiotic relationship between seasonal festivity and peasant rebels who adopted mock king titles, organizing their defiance of government into festive patterns. The questions and answers which have resulted have radically altered critical views as to the "safety valve" theory of festive games.'[26] That is, work in this area has shown how the imagery of misrule could be used for a variety of social and political ends, rather than just acting to reinforce the status quo.

The view of misrule which is found in this literature contrasts markedly with that which occurs in studies of individual customs. The view here is that the exceptional nature of festive behaviour reinforces the general rule of law and authority during the rest of the year. For example, in a review of the evidence for the custom of hocking in England, Sally-Beth MacLean cites Natalie Zemon Davis's view that play with images of 'women on top' offers a temporary release from stable hierarchy, as well as being part of the conflict to change the basic distribution of power within society.[27] By 'women on top', Davis is referring to images and symbols in which women have the mastery or upper hand, such as stories about Amazons or Phyllis riding Aristotle, or the painful representations of women thrashing men's backsides found for example on playing cards.[28] MacLean observes that 'Hocktide may provide some evidence of this conflict, but in the medieval context at least, it does not seem to have been an agent of social change.'[29] Similarly, in a paper in the same volume, Peter Greenfield suggests that Christmas drama in aristocratic households, which 'presumably involved elements of carnival inversion and travesty of social order and authority', was in fact a means of reaffirming the authority of the lord over his household and the surrounding countryside. '[T]he English aristocracy of the fifteenth, sixteenth, and early seventeenth centuries seem to have enjoyed the plays of local amateurs at Christmas time, perhaps not just because there was no slander in these allowed fools, but also perhaps because in the very act of allowing, and in the performing of what is allowed, authority is exercised and reaffirmed.'[30] A final example is Claire Sponsler's discussion of morris dancing and her consideration of the way in which it might function as a ritual staging of illicit or proscribed activities:

> However, because the festive misrule of morris dancing took place as part of the symbolic labor of feasts, ceremonies, gift-exchanges, visits, and other rituals of reciprocal relations, it worked toward reproducing established relations as much as toward overthrowing them, no matter how much it contested orthodoxy. For this reason, festivities of misrule were, perhaps not surprisingly, rarely genuinely subversive and were in fact most often deeply conservative ... Especially within the context of civic processions, court revels, and parish games, festive disorder in large part reaffirmed authority, offering reassurances about authority's ability to contain disorder and resolving it in a final image of unity and concord.[31]

Morris dancing and misrule both are understood to be temporarily subversive but ultimately conservative in the way that
they play with social norms and expectations.

It should be clear then that as with the secondary literature
on ritual and ceremony in medieval English towns, there are a
number of opposing views about why misrule is actually performed, and how it worked, in accounts of medieval drama and
calendar customs. Again, this range of views causes difficulties
when we try to reach an overview of the situation, or want to
know how to go about investigating some new evidence that has
come to light. Should all mentions of hocking be interpreted as
socially conservative? What situations might produce different
kinds of meanings? As has already been suggested in the
previous section, the difficulties posed by these kinds of
questions can in part be resolved by approaching the question
of misrule's function with an open mind: it makes little sense to
prejudge the outcome of a particular performance prior to
looking at the specifics of that situation. A further issue that can
be raised here is the question of why medieval people should
want to get involved in such activities in the first place, that is,
the motivation behind misrule. Several of the views considered
in this section describe misrule as 'subversive'. This may be
interpreted as saying that by making use of images and practices
which broke with social norms the participants were seeking to
undermine or change the present state of society: women
hockers threatening to tie men up for example. Although this
might be true of some examples, a wider range of possible
intentions must surely be imagined – clowning around in a
Christmas play need be no more than harmless fun, and a way of
bringing the events of one's faith to life through drama for
example.

So again, we have a situation where the theoretical model
appears to be driving the interpretation, narrowing down the
range of meanings which might be found in the evidence,
although this time it is happening in relation to motivation
rather than outcome. One way out of this situation is to suggest
that although misrule certainly makes use of inversion, this does

not necessarily mean that it was being employed in a controversial or dissident way. In fact, inversion can be used for a variety of purposes, and it is important to be aware of this. For example, in respect of Sponsler's discussion, while it is possible, although perhaps difficult, to imagine that 'the festive misrule of morris dancing' could on occasion be potentially subversive and contest orthodoxy, these meanings need not have characterised every performance; if they did, it would hardly have been so widely practised or enjoyed. The crucial point here is that the kinds of inversion which characterise festive misrule need not have always been politically motivated. Rather, inversion is a technique which can be deployed for a range of purposes; from sheer enjoyment to a means of punishing those who are perceived to have stepped out of line, as well as for expressing opposition to the existing norms of society. In those instances where festive misrule did have a politically contentious dimension, this was a choice made by the people involved, or caused by the authorities treating it as seditious or rebellious; it is not however an intrinsic property of the genre. In conclusion, it is clear that when analysing any particular example of misrule, an open mind must be kept about the motivations and interests behind that performance, until its specifics have been explored. An appreciation of the variable intentions for misrule is thus a second aspect of the more effective approach to medieval misrule which will be discussed in the next chapter.

Wider approaches to medieval misrule: Bakhtin and carnival

It is a notable irony that at the same time as scholars working on the Middle Ages have lamented the marginality of their discipline, a substantial part of the rest of the academic world appear to have been taking a vigorous interest in that very period.[32] In fact ideas about carnival and its medieval incarnations are everywhere in cultural studies and related areas, being used to explain phenomena as diverse as car-boot sales and rock and roll. The popularity of this approach owes much to the influence of the Russian scholar Mikhail Bakhtin, whose exuberant descriptions of the festive life of the Middle Ages have concentrated critical minds on how popular culture might work as a force for political change. Unfortunately the attractiveness of Bakhtin's prose, and in particular its focus upon what is euphemistically translated as the 'material bodily lower stratum', tends to belie its poor substantiation at the level of the historical evidence. A number of recent studies have therefore raised questions about Bakhtin's notion of carnival in the terms of the sources that were available to him when he wrote. For instance, in a review of Bakhtin's work on Rabelais, Richard Berrong asks:

> What, one might or should ask, are Bakhtin's sources, his basis for so extensive and elaborate a description of popular culture? One will have to keep on asking, I'm afraid. Bakhtin indicates very few primary sources, and one often has the impression that his 'medieval and Renaissance popular culture' is largely an amalgamation of Goethe's notes on an eighteenth-century Venetian carnival and Bakhtin's own preconception of what that popular culture should have been.[33]

In spite of these limitations, there remains a continuing enthusiasm for Bakhtin's work. In this section some examples of the way that Bakhtin's accounts of medieval festive culture has been taken up and used in cultural studies and literary analysis will be considered.

The details of Bakhtin's lengthy career and the extraordinary conditions under which he worked for much of his life make for fascinating reading, and they do not easily lend themselves to a concise summary.[34] Suffice to say that the terrible privations which Bakhtin endured during his life give his celebration of the popular culture of the people an extra resonance.[35] There are two works in English translation in which Bakhtin considers carnival and the specific forms that it took in the medieval and Renaissance periods. The most well-known of these is *Rabelais and his World*, originally Bakhtin's doctoral dissertation and revised for publication in 1965, with an English translation appearing in 1968. The other work is *Problems of Dostoevsky's*

Poetics, the English translation of the second edition being published in 1973.[36] It is worth emphasising that Bakhtin does not set out in either of these books to investigate carnival itself; rather, he reconstructs it as a way of helping to explain the particular characteristics of the writings of these two authors. In *Problems of Dostoevsky's Poetics*, Bakhtin uses the term 'carnival' to denote particular qualities that literature and festival life have in common, stretching back to antiquity. His concern is to identify how elements of carnival culture have come to be transposed into literature:

> Literature that was influenced – directly and without mediation, or indirectly, through a series of intermediate links – by one or another variant of carnivalistic folklore (ancient or medieval) we shall call *carnivalized literature*. The entire realm of the serio-comical constitutes the first example of such literature. In our opinion the problem of carnivalized literature is one of the very important problems in historical poetics, and in particular of the poetics of genre.
>
> ...
>
> The problem of *carnival* (in the sense of the sum total of all diverse festivities, rituals and forms of a carnival type) – its essence, its deep roots in the primordial order and the primordial thinking of man, its development under conditions of class society, its extraordinary life force and its undying fascination – is one of the most complex and most interesting problems in the history of culture. We cannot, of course, do justice to it here. What interests us here is essentially only the problem of carnivalization, that is, the determining influence of carnival on literature and more precisely on literary genre.[37]

For Bakhtin there are a number of 'carnivalistic categories' that were transposed over thousands of years from carnival forms into literature, including a lack of distinction between actors and spectators, the suspension of hierarchical differences between people, a free and familiar attitude towards the world, and profanation.[38] Having established this general thesis, Bakhtin examines how it was played out in different historical periods; thus, *Rabelais and his World* is an exploration of the influence of medieval and Renaissance carnival on the writings of this author. Bakhtin's description of medieval carnival is dispersed throughout the book, but he does include a concise summary of what he perceives its main features to have been in *Problems of Dostoevsky's Poetics*:

> In the Middle Ages the vast comic and parodic literature in vernacular languages and in Latin was, one way or another, connected with festivals of the carnival type – with carnival proper, with the 'Festival of Fools', with free 'paschal laughter' (*risus paschalis*), and so forth. Essentially every church holiday in the Middle Ages had its carnivalistic side, the side facing the public square (especially those holidays like Corpus Christi). Many national festivities, such as the bullfight, for example, were of a clearly expressed carnivalistic character. A carnival atmosphere reigned during the days of a fair, on the festival of the harvesting of grapes, on the performance days of miracle plays, mystery plays, *soties* and so forth; the entire theatrical life of the Middle Ages was carnivalistic ... It could be said (with certain reservations, of course) that a person of the Middle Ages lived, as it were, *two lives*: one was the *official* life, monolithically serious and gloomy, subjugated to a strict hierarchical order, full of terror, dogmatism, reverence, and piety; the other was the *life of the carnival square*, free and unrestricted, full of ambivalent laughter, blasphemy, the profanation of everything sacred, full of debasing and obscenities, familiar contact with everyone and everything. Both these lives were legitimate, but separated by strict temporal boundaries.[39]

It should be clear from this description that Bakhtin uses the term 'carnival' in a very wide sense indeed. The main point to draw out is the idea that medieval people occupied something close to two separate worlds, one official and one unofficial, and that the latter was defined by its carnival character. In the light of how Bakhtin's ideas have been taken up, it is worth noting that he does distinguish between the pleasures of carnival and practical attempts to change the social order, writing that it would be 'a mistake to presume that popular distrust of seriousness and popular love of laugher, as of another truth, could

31

always reach full awareness, expressing a critical and clearly defined opposition.'[40]

Many critics have taken Bakhtin's description of carnival as an objective account of the festival culture of the Middle Ages, using it as a standard against which to compare the popular culture of later historical periods, especially that of the present day. In such accounts medieval carnival is usually rather nostalgically represented, appearing as a scandalous and topsy-turvy occasion on which ordinary folk enjoyed the chance to mock their rulers and show off their bottoms. This point of view sees the utopian world of medieval carnival as being gradually suppressed over the centuries, leaving us with a bland, neutered and commercialised popular culture in the present day. For example, Tony Bennett uses carnival as a yardstick against which to measure a particular experience of Blackpool Pleasure Beach:

> For Bakhtin, the carnival of the late medieval period was not just a festival of transgression. It was characterised by the inversion not just of everyday rules and behaviour, but of the dominant symbolic order. As his study of Rabelais makes clear, carnival was a festival of *discrowning* in which the axial signifiers of medieval ideology were scandalously and often scatologically debased … The Pleasure Beach is simply not like that, not even remotely. The body may be whirled upside down, hurled this way and that, but, in the coding of these pleasures for consumption, the dominant symbolic order remains solidly intact and unwaveringly the right way up.[41]

Carnival has also been used as the point of comparison for many other aspects of contemporary popular culture.[42] When medieval carnival is cited in this comparative way, it is not often backed up with reference to actual historical examples: the enthusiasm of particular critics for the Middle Ages sounds rather hollow when it is clear that they are unfamiliar with any of the substantial research that has been done in this area since Bakhtin or C. L. Barber were writing. In the rarer instances where actual examples are cited, they are invariably drawn from

Le Roy Ladurie's discussion of Carnival in Romans from the later sixteenth century, without any awareness that what might hold for France is not necessarily true for England or indeed anywhere else. This is not just a matter of keeping up with the latest research, it is about the more fundamental issue of the circumstances under which historical comparisons between cultures five hundred years apart can be useful or even valid.

Other commentators have taken a more sceptical line on carnival, seeing its excesses as easily tolerated by those in authority, since any critical potential was undermined precisely because it took place within the narrow confines of the festive holiday. Carnival may have been exceptional but it also proved the general rule. For example, Umberto Eco writes that:

> Carnival can exist only as an *authorized* transgression (which in fact represents a blatant case of *contradictio in adjectio* or of happy *double binding* – capable of curing instead of producing neurosis). If the ancient, religious carnival was limited in time, the modern mass-carnival is limited in space: it is reserved for certain places, certain streets, or framed by the television screen.
>
> In this sense, comedy and carnival are not instances of real transgressions: on the contrary, they represent paramount examples of law reinforcement. They remind us of the existence of the rule.[43]

We can also mention Terry Eagleton's often-cited remarks regarding Bakhtin and carnival from his discussion of the work of Walter Benjamin. Eagleton observes that '[i]ndeed carnival is so vivaciously celebrated that the necessary political criticism is almost too obvious to make. Carnival, after all, is a *licensed* affair in every sense, a permissible rupture of hegemony, a contained popular blow-off as disturbing and relatively ineffectual as a revolutionary work of art.'[44]

From this short discussion a familiar set of oppositions emerge. Carnival has been seen as either something radical and opposed to conventional notions of decency and order, or as an ultimately conservative phenomenon, since showing off your bottom in public, while admittedly fun, doesn't tend to free people from the shackles of whichever economic system binds them. If this opposition between social protest and safety-valve is already familiar to us, then so are the limitations of these approaches as a means of answering the questions posed at the beginning of this chapter. That said, in this area of scholarship the routes to a more constructive line of enquiry have been discussed in some detail. For example, Simon Dentith has usefully summarised the historical arguments against the idea of a wholly anti-authoritarian carnival culture, proposing instead a more pluralist approach to the evidence. After a discussion of Le Roy Ladurie's work in the context of Bakhtin's view of carnival, Dentith concludes that '[t]he carnival at Romans, therefore, suggests not that the carnivalesque has one univocal social or political meaning, but that it provides a malleable space, in which activities and symbols can be inflected in different directions'.[45] In addition, Peter Stallybrass and Allon White have sought to move the terms of debate away from an apparent choice between the polarised viewpoints of subversion or containment, by means of a historical investigation of the theme of transgression:

> It actually makes little sense to fight out the issue of whether or not carnivals are *intrinsically* radical or conservative, for to do so automatically involves the false essentializing of carnivalesque transgression. The most that can be said in the abstract is that for long periods carnival may be a stable and cyclical ritual with no noticeable politically transformative effects but that, given the presence of sharpened political antagonism, it may often act as *catalyst* and *site of actual and symbolic struggle*.[46]

Assembling an extraordinarily wide range of evidence, both historically and socially, Stallybrass and White are able to demonstrate that carnival-style practices are only one of a range of cultural forms that make use of the inversion or intermingling of social categories. In terms of the analysis of particular examples therefore, the implication is that the emphasis should be upon investigation rather than comparison, with the aim being to explore what is distinctive about each particular example.

In conclusion, it is clear that while most opinion has been divided between the familiar perspectives of radicalism or safety-valve in cultural studies, the limitations of both these approaches have also been recognised. There are two points which are relevant to our consideration of how we might refine our approach to the study of festive misrule, and popular culture more generally. First, as a review of some of the secondary literature relating to Bakhtin's work has shown, many of the common generalisations about misrule are based upon assumptions about the evidence, rather than proceeding from an actual analysis of it. In terms of an approach to new sources therefore, a close study offers the best way forward, since it not only makes fuller use of the historical evidence, but also sees this kind of analysis as the key to a fuller understanding of culture and social process. A second point which follows from Stallybrass and White's discussion is their notion of 'transgression', as a way of describing how cultural symbolism can be turned upside down or inside out. This is a term which is particularly useful for discussing medieval misrule, since it characterises what is distinctive about practices of this sort, namely the manipulation of cultural categories or imagery in some way, without making a comment about their intention or function, as terms like 'subversion' tend to do. Overall, the more progressive work in this area has emphasised the importance of a contextual over a comparative approach, and has developed terminology which is more generally applicable to practices of this type. This method and terminology will form part of the new approach to misrule which is outlined in chapter 2.

Conclusion

This chapter has explored the secondary literature on the festive misrule of medieval England, showing some of the main trends and arguments. The accompanying discussion has suggested that we cannot realistically know or deduce the meaning of misrule merely by reference to explanatory models like that of the safety-valve approach. Instead it is more appropriate and constructive to investigate the function of a custom through a closer study of its context and effects. Clearly, if the meanings of particular occurrences are to be analysed and compared, the methodology which we adopt must enable us to deal with the characteristics which are common to a range of customs, as well as making it possible to appreciate what is different about each individual occurrence. This new methodology will be my concern in the next chapter.

Notes

1 Scott, *Domination and the Arts of Resistance*, p. 177.
2 See Burke, *Popular Culture in Early Modern Europe*, Davis, *Society and Culture in Early Modern France* and Le Roy Ladurie, *Carnival*.
3 For recent discussions of the relationships between carnival and medieval/ early modern literature see Cook, 'Carnival and *The Canterbury Tales*', Hall, 'Carnival and history' and the collection of essays edited by Farrell, *Bakhtin and Medieval Voices*.
4 Phythian-Adams, 'Ceremony and the citizen'; reprinted in Rosser and Holt (eds), *The Medieval Town*. All subsequent references will be to the original 1972 edition of this essay.
5 Phythian-Adams, 'Ceremony and the citizen', pp. 66 and 69–70.
6 Phythian-Adams, *Local History and Folklore*, pp. 26–7.
7 James, 'Ritual, drama and social body', p. 4.
8 James, 'Ritual, drama and social body', pp. 11 and 15.
9 Womack, 'Imagining communities', p. 98.
10 Lindenbaum, 'Rituals of exclusion', pp. 54–5.
11 Lindenbaum, 'Rituals of exclusion', pp. 55 and 63 n. 6.
12 Lindenbaum, 'Rituals of exclusion', pp. 59–60.
13 See Lindenbaum, 'The Smithfield tournament of 1390', pp. 1–2 and 'Ceremony and oligarchy'. Ruth Evans argues that James ignores sexual difference as an area of tension and division in late medieval urban society in her essay, 'Body politics'. See also Rubin, *Corpus Christi*, pp. 265–7 and the introduction to Phythian-Adams, 'Ceremony and the citizen', in Rosser and Holt (eds), *The Medieval Town*, pp. 238–9.
14 Phythian-Adams, 'Ceremony and the citizen', pp. 58–9.
15 Hanawalt, *Growing Up in Medieval London*, pp. 125–6.
16 Camille, *Image on the Edge*, p. 143. For a critical appraisal of this book see the review by Hamburger in *The Art Bulletin* 75.
17 Phythian-Adams, *Local History and Folklore*, p. 26.

18 Justice, *Writing and Rebellion*, pp. 153–4 nn. 55–7 (p. 153).

19 Justice, *Writing and Rebellion*, pp. 154 and 154–5.

20 See for example Dyer, 'The Rising of 1381 in Suffolk', p. 281 and chapter 4 of the present book.

21 Lancashire, *Dramatic Texts and Records of Britain*, pp. 62 and 232.

22 Happé, *English Drama before Shakespeare*, p. 2.

23 Hutton, *Rise and Fall of Merry England*, p. 2.

24 See Bercé, *Fête et Révolte*, Davis, *Society and Culture in Early Modern France* and Le Roy Ladurie, *Carnival*.

25 Gash, 'Carnival against Lent', p. 81.

26 Billington, *Mock Kings in Medieval Society and Renaissance Drama*, p. 1.

27 MacLean, 'Hocktide: a reassessment', pp. 238–9.

28 Davis, 'Women on top', pp. 156, 158 and 162.

29 MacLean, 'Hocktide: a reassessment', p. 239.

30 Greenfield, 'Festive drama at Christmas', pp. 34 and 38.

31 Sponsler, 'Writing the unwritten', p. 86.

32 Patterson, 'On the margin', p. 87.

33 Berrong, *Rabelais and Bakhtin*, pp. 128–9 n. 11. For other critiques see Gurevich, '"High and low": the medieval grotesque', Klaniczay, 'The carnival spirit', Davidson, 'Carnival, Lent and drama' and Humphrey, 'Bakhtin and popular culture'.

34 See Clark and Holquist, *Mikhail Bakhtin*.

35 See Brandist, *Carnival Culture and the Soviet Modernist Novel*.

36 Clark and Holquist, *Mikhail Bakhtin*, pp. 354–5. The English translations I have used are M. Bakhtin, *Rabelais and his World*, trans. H. Iswolsky, Bloomington, 1984 and Bakhtin, *Problems of Dostoevsky's Poetics*, trans. and ed. C. Emerson, Theory and History of Literature 8, Manchester, 1984. All subsequent references are to these editions.

37 Bakhtin, *Problems of Dostoevsky's Poetics*, pp. 107 and 122.

38 Bakhtin, *Problems of Dostoevsky's Poetics*, pp. 122–3.

39 Bakhtin, *Problems of Dostoevsky's Poetics*, pp. 129–30.

40 Bakhtin, *Rabelais and his World*, p. 95.

41 Bennett, 'A thousand and one troubles', p. 153. Emphasis in original.

42 See for example Gregson and Crewe, 'The bargain, the knowledge, and the spectacle' and Kohl, 'Looking through a glass onion'. For a discussion of the limitations of these kinds of comparisons see Humphrey, 'Bakhtin and popular culture'.

43 Eco, 'The frames of comic "freedom"', p. 6. Emphasis in original.

44 Eagleton, *Walter Benjamin*, p. 148.

45 Dentith, *Bakhtinian Thought*, pp. 74–6 (p. 75).

46 Stallybrass and White, *Politics and Poetics of Transgression*, pp. 11–14 (p. 14). Emphasis in original.

2

A new approach to the study
of medieval misrule

Introduction

Imagine picking up a newspaper and reading the headline: 'Archaeologists announce discovery of ancient race of skeleton people.' It wouldn't take long to realise what was going on here – either it was April Fools' Day, or this particular bunch of archaeologists had overlooked a fundamental principle governing the interpretation of the past. This example shows that any kind of research or investigation involves more than just digging, reading or measuring something new; it also means thinking very carefully about what can plausibly be said about the evidence that is found. There are a range of conventions that govern such interpretations, and they may be expressed in academic terms or as just plain common sense: in relation to the 'race of skeleton people' story for instance, a non-archaeologist can plainly see the weakness of this conclusion. It would take a brave or foolhardy person to argue that a set of bones found by archaeologists showed that a race of skeleton people once existed, but then many discoveries or breakthroughs have sounded totally implausible at first. Where they stand or fall is whether the leap from evidence to interpretation turns out to be a credible one.

What chapter 1 showed was that many academic discussions of festive misrule do in fact fail this test of plausibility, and for fairly simple reasons. All too often interpretation is simply a matter of slotting the evidence into the categories of an pre-existing model, rather than taking the time to study it further, and think constructively about the conclusions that one reaches. Given this situation, this chapter aims to set out a view of misrule which provides both a credible description of what misrule is, and an approach which enables us to make best sense of new evidence when we come across it. The basic definition of misrule that was proposed in the Introduction will be elaborated upon first, in order to come up with a secure and properly thought-out means of characterising festive misrule's main features. The second part of this chapter will lay out a new set of guidelines for the effective study of misrule in the historical record. As should be clear, the underlying approach developed here is one which owes much to literary techniques of reading and argument, and to an understanding of misrule which treats it as performance rather than as a ritual or rebellion. Some ideas from anthropology and from social science are also used, in the belief that there are many fruitful points of contact between anthropology and the study of contemporary and historical performance, a link which this book hopes to encourage further.[1] Overall the aim is to provide a constructive alternative to the explicit reliance on the work of earlier anthropologists like Gluckman, whose ideas about 'rituals of rebellion' continue to influence the study of misrule, despite the fact that they are largely discredited within anthropology itself.[2]

There are several practical guides to the study of popular festivity and drama which can complement the suggestions outlined in this chapter. In *Local History and Folklore*, a slim volume which is little known but deserves to be widely read, Charles Phythian-Adams has set out an extremely helpful guide to the study of popular practices, including an outline of the four interrelated facets of social customs prior to the Reformation. These are considered to be the context of popular beliefs, the physical location of customs, their calendrical timing and their social function; a section is also devoted to the analysis of source material.[3] This framework has been influential in the approach to festive misrule which is outlined here. Also valuable is Meg Twycross's introduction to *Festive Drama*, a collection of essays on early European drama, customs and processions.

Twycross makes use of a distinction between theatre history, where the concern is with the 'rhetoric' of an occasion, the ways in which its contents are arranged and presented, and cultural history, where the interest is in its social function and meaning.[4] This distinction is useful for characterising the different kinds of approaches that have been taken to misrule. Furthermore, Twycross offers some excellent suggestions regarding analysis, which include ensuring that we have all the available evidence before we interpret a performance, considering the practicalities of performance, and taking into account the 'Small Catastrophe Theory', that is, the differences between the plan and how an event actually turns out – we must remember that in practice devils accidentally caught on fire, giants got decapitated and on numerous occasions rain stopped play.[5] These suggestions stand in addition to the proposals that are put forward in this chapter. The discussion ranges over a number of areas of enquiry, with the result that the field of secondary reference is potentially very large indeed. In order to keep the main text and the notes to a manageable length, not all of the relevant secondary sources are cited, and further references are given in the notes.

Definitions

So far in this book the term 'festive misrule' has been used to describe any custom which took place at a well-defined time of the year, and which turned upside-down or broke with established rules or norms in some way. This definition has usefully captured when these customs took place, and has expressed the essential features that they had in common. However, chapter 1 showed that there are further issues that have interested people about misrule, including why such customs are performed in the first place, and what it is they actually accomplish. It was clear that there were a number of conflicting answers to these questions, ranging from the idea that such occasions expressed radical social ideas, through to the notion that misrule is just a safety-valve which dissipated resentment. Since these ideas proved on closer inspection to be too general or too prescriptive, what we really need is a way of thinking about and defining misrule which captures its essence, and yet which also enables us to talk about its cultural role in a way which recognises diversity. A very useful means of expressing both of these qualities can be taken from Peter Stallybrass and Allon White's book *The Politics and Poetics of Transgression*, where this question of function is addressed.

As we have already seen, this book considers Bakhtin's work and the scholarly debate about the radical or conservative nature of carnival. However, the book also contains some interesting ideas about how to characterise carnival, suggesting that carnival occasions are not the only time or place where conventional roles and symbols can be mixed up or inverted. In fact many different areas of culture can display what the anthropologist Barbara Babcock calls 'symbolic inversion', defined as 'any act of expressive behaviour which inverts, contradicts, abrogates, or in some fashion presents an alternative to commonly held cultural codes, values, and norms be they linguistic, literary or artistic, religious, or social and political'.[6] As one example Stallybrass and White point to the women protestors who occupied makeshift tents on common land outside of Greenham Common nuclear missile base near Newbury, Berkshire in the 1980s and 1990s; here, many traditional and established notions such as gender roles and rights to land use were deliberately breached in the course of the protest.[7]

What makes the idea of symbolic inversion so useful for talking about festive misrule in the Middle Ages is that it enables us to capture the central feature of these customs, the quality that they all had in common, while at the same time leaving open the questions of motivation or outcomes that have tended to cloud the issue. As we have seen, misrule relies upon the self-conscious decision of individuals to perform in ways which are somehow contrary to social expectations, but these performances varied enormously in their meaning, from a bishop choosing to sit in the choir-stalls whilst a chorister leads the procession to high altar, to the blatant theft of a whole tree from private land for the purposes of building a maypole. So instead of loading our interpretation in advance, as terms such as 'subversion' or 'disorder' tend to do, we need to be able to say that custom A or ritual B involves some kind of inversion, and reserve our judgement of what that achieves for a closer analysis. This is why a term like 'symbolic inversion', or as Stallybrass and White prefer, 'transgression', is so useful, since it expresses what is distinctive about misrule, without squeezing it into some wider theory or class of actions. 'Transgression' is an interesting choice: although it has an oppositional sense in general usage, it should be regarded as neutral with respect to purpose in this context, so that to transgress is to break the boundaries or mix up elements of culture that are supposed to be kept separate.[8] Describing festive misrule as a genre of performance which makes strong use of the theme of transgression captures what all instances have in common, while leaving us room to consider the use to which it is put in particular cases.

This approach also focuses our attention on the question of how transgression is actually produced in the first place, since if misrule is to work successfully, the boundaries or standards that are being overstepped must be reasonably clear to the performers, and the audience. Here we can make use of recent thinking about the 'performative' way in which individuals observe social norms. That is, an arguably more productive way of thinking about social norms is that rather than existing as some prior and monolithic structure which then determines the way that individuals behave, such norms emerge precisely because they are constantly performed and reiterated as such.[9] Once we begin to think about misrule as transgression, it is clear that we start with a number of blanks that we need to fill in, such as where the sense of transgression actually derives from, its nature and scale, and the reasons and interests motivating it. By answering these questions, an occasion of misrule is seen as an individual and dynamic cultural performance in its own right, as opposed to just another manifestation of a type whose characteristics are apparently already known in advance. It also enables us to explain how people in the Middle Ages could wilfully misconstrue misrule, either by trying to pass off their obviously antisocial actions as 'harmless fun', or by claiming that someone else's benign pursuit was in fact a flagrant moral outrage: transgression is most certainly in the eye of the beholder.

A third advantage of this approach is that it gives us a way of talking about how misrule relates to apparently similar kinds of cultural activity, without lumping them all together under a generalised heading, as terms such as 'the carnivalesque' tends to do. For example, misrule is often discussed alongside ritual-ised forms of punishment known as 'charivari', where social behaviour which has overstepped certain boundaries is punished through the imaginative humiliation of a victim.[10] One such form of public punishment in this period was to place an individual on horseback and parade them about the local area facing towards the tail-end of the beast.[11] At York in 1536 for instance, a husband and wife who admitted to posting slander-ous bills around the town were set on horseback, facing the horse's tail, and led about the streets.[12] The similarities with misrule are evident, but there are substantial differences too: in the case described the recipients were presumably unwilling to take part and the punishments were meted out by local officials; furthermore, the sense of transgression is personal and individual rather than making reference to any higher authority such as a monarch, which is a characteristic of misrule. So the advantage of using a term like transgression in its purely neutral sense is that it is able to capture what both misrule and charivari share, while avoiding any implication that they were closely related kinds of activity. Not only that, but if misrule is just one example of where inversions are used in culture, then our attention is drawn to the reasons why people should tend to think in terms of high and low, or top and bottom, and what it means to break with these categories.

Investigating social and political meanings

As we have seen, it is essential that we use the correct words and concepts for defining misrule. This emphasis on precision also applies to thinking about what misrule does, because an incorrect term may colour or prejudge how we think about its meaning too. For instance if custom X is characterised from the outset as something like 'legitimized disorder', this does not exactly encourage an interpretation which sees it as producing a sense of community pride, which it may well do: how do we know until we take a closer look?[13] Although the idea of transgression helps us to avoid prejudging meaning in this way, it doesn't really tell us about how we actually go about researching the meaning and function of particular customs. In fact, apart from the studies by Phythian-Adams and Twycross mentioned earlier, there is not much written that can help with this task. In the second part of this chapter therefore, the basic steps which any good analysis should take are set out. There are three main stages to go through: first, an assessment of the evidence; second, some careful thought about possible roles; and third, a consideration of how a particular example might fit into wider cultural trends and movements. Each of these areas will be considered in turn.

As an example to assist our thinking, we can imagine that our interest is in the role of women in popular culture in England in the Middle Ages, and that we are wanting to investigate in more detail a reference from the churchwardens' accounts of the church of St Mary at Hill, London, in 1498: 'Item, for iij Rybbes of bief to the wyves on hokmonday, & for ale & bred for them that gaderyd ... Summa, xvjd.'[14] What this entry says is that 16d. was paid for beef, bread and ale for the wives who collected money through hocking on the Hock Monday of that year. We already know something about what hocking was, and this entry looks like a celebratory meal to accompany the occasion, perhaps because an unusually large amount of money was collected in this year. How might we find out, and how can we investigate the role of the custom in this particular parish, and the part that women played in it? These are questions that will be addressed in the course of the discussion.

Evidence

The first stage in any analysis must be to understand fully the nature of the evidence, and to appreciate what may reasonably be inferred from it and what cannot. This means looking closely at the medium in which a reference occurs, and seeing whether the reference is unique, part of a longer tradition, or perhaps the first or last mention in that source. In the case of the example given above, this reference to hocking appears in a set of churchwardens accounts which can easily be tracked down: these accounts were edited by Littlehales in the Early English Text Society series as *The Medieval Records of a London City Church (St. Mary at Hill) A.D. 1420–1559*.[15] A closer look at these accounts shows that our reference occurs as part of a continuous run of entries between 1496 and 1515, when receipts from hocking are recorded in most years; in addition there are other isolated references to money being collected in 1524 and 1527. Although the women of the parish do not seem to have collected an unusually large sum of money in 1498 when they had their meal, in the previous year they did amass one of their highest totals: perhaps the two things are related, but perhaps not.[16] In fact we are unlikely to find out because these records had a very specific purpose, which was to record financial transactions, rather than explain why they were made, and the more general point to make is that our view of any custom is always going to be limited by the kind of record in which it is mentioned. This means that what we say about the evidence must be thought out and properly justified.

A second point to make is that by definition, the evidence that we deal with was recorded by someone for particular reasons, which may or may not be explicit. Even if the motives for writing are apparently self-evident, such as the records of a council meeting or a judicial verdict, we still need to approach them with a certain amount of healthy scepticism prior to any closer analysis. Although it is often said that all records are 'biased', this doesn't quite capture the kind of awareness that we need to cultivate. It is less a matter of trying to see how accounts might diverge from a central truth, and more a case of trying to understand the cultural baggage and presuppositions that lead to a particular way of representing people and events. For instance, women are often not named in medieval documents, and instead appear in relation to their husbands, fathers, masters or brothers, such as 'the wife of John Smith'. This is not really due to bias in the usual sense of this word, but rather reflects a whole cultural way of perceiving the role of women in public life. In fact it is unlikely that medieval England was really filled with the nameless and anonymous women who loom large in the surviving records, and more probable that this represents a particular way of judging, classifying and representing women of which we need to take account. Clearly, these kinds of issues are especially acute for contentious areas of social life like misrule, where multiple and conflicting opinions of events are the norm. As Alan Somerset has usefully advised in a study which explores these questions for a disputed festive occasion in Shrewsbury in 1591, we should be careful about crediting the rhetoric that we find in the records as giving us the full explanation of what actually happened.[17]

This discussion of the limitations and inclinations of the evidence may make the prospect of looking for social meanings appear rather gloomy, but this need not be the case: while it is sensible to err on the side of caution, it can be surprising how much can be said about some kinds of issues. Taking a wider view of hocking in the St Mary at Hill records, an interesting point is they show that while the women hocked on Hock Monday, the men of the parish took their revenge on the next day, Hock Tuesday. Not only that, but where separate sums of money are recorded, the women's total always exceeds the men's by at least twice as much each year. So hocking in this parish was about a lot more than just a 'safety-valve': it was an occasion on which women, or more specifically the unnamed 'wives', might collect and donate reasonable sums of money to their parish church, certainly more than the men of the parish.

And from this observation we can begin to think about what this meant for parish life in general; what role did an annual bout of hocking play in the life of the community? At this point we can start to read more widely about the parish or village or town in which our custom is taking place: for instance there are several publications about the medieval parish of St Mary at Hill, including an article by Clive Burgess and a book by Paul Jeffery.[18] Descriptive accounts like these help to bring the rather abstract records to life, showing the men and women mentioned in the records as more than just performers: they also had to earn a living, or keep a family, which affected how they took part in festivity. To sum up, our starting point is always going to be a mention of an instance of misrule in a document or a text. Taking a critical view of that evidence, in terms of deciding what it can and cannot tell us, is a vital first step in the investigation of the social meaning of a custom.

Meanings and outcomes

The next step in our analysis is to form a view of what the meaning and outcomes of that instance of misrule might be, where possible. So far we have been careful to approach misrule through fairly neutral and open-minded terminology, and this commitment goes so far as appreciating that even the same kind of custom can have a variety of possible meanings, depending upon who is taking part and when it happens. For instance, if a soccer World Cup Final match excited the same passions as a Sunday league kick-about, it would be disastrous for international football. In fact, even if the same custom takes place in very similar conditions over consecutive years, with the same individuals involved, the meaning of consecutive performances may still vary, as a sense of tradition develops for instance. So with these points in mind, what range of possible meanings are we looking out for? Although anything which may be construed as a kind of 'checklist' of possible functions is undesirable, it is useful to set out the range of different circumstances in which misrule is found, in order to illustrate the diversity of meanings that it might have.

Probably the most difficult context to appreciate festive misrule taking place is when it occurs in a religious setting, such in medieval parish churches, monasteries and cathedrals. It is not always easy to see how misrule might be accommodated within the sober and respectful atmosphere that we usually associate with these spaces. That said, the use of reversal and inversions in religious ritual and custom is just one part of a wider 'world upside-down' theme associated with medieval religion, and which also includes the grotesque images found in margins of manuscripts, and in the decoration of stonework and choir-stalls in churches.[19] This was an important aesthetic in its own right: opposites, inversions and reversals were not automatically excluded from public representation in this period, but carried messages which demonstrated morality or folly, as well as subjects to provoke healthy laughter. In terms of misrule, there were several customs associated with important festival periods that depended for their significance on some sort of inversion or breach of religious decorum. Examples from medieval Europe include the boy-bishop and the Feast of Fools. Although the purpose of such practices was not always clear to contemporary or later commentators, it is possible to make a sensible case for why they were used. As Eamon Duffy notes of the boy-bishop custom, '[a] perfectly good Christian justification could be offered for these popular observances, however close to the bone their elements of parody and misrule brought them: Christ's utterances about children and the Kingdom of Heaven, Isaiah's prophecy that a little child shall lead them, and the theme of inversion and the world turned upside-down found in texts like the "Magnificat" could all be invoked in their defence'.[20] This kind of generalised explanation is very useful in that it prevents such practices from being regarded merely as forms of opposition to a more austere church doctrine: in fact, the boy-bishop custom can be seen as perfectly exemplifying religious teaching about humility and salvation. That said, the limitations of such an explanation in the analysis of particular cases also needs to be recognised: in the thirteenth and fourteenth centuries prominent churchmen complained that boisterous activities such as mud-slinging, playing pranks and praising demons were taking place in churches and cathedrals at Christmas, suggesting that not all misrule was tolerated or even understood.[21]

Among all the erudite scholarly discussion of misrule's meaning and social significance, it can be easy to overlook the fact that play with classificatory categories was and continues to be something enjoyable and worth pursuing for this end alone. Although this can of course be done at any time of the year, we are interested here in customs which are associated with particular periods in the calendar. Christmas was the most obvious example, with even the higher echelons of society being willing to indulge in festive humour and hilarity. Olga Horner's account of Christmas entertainments at the Inns of Court contains plenty of examples of what can be designated as transgressive behaviour among gentlemen who went on to assume prominent positions at court. At the Inner Temple we find that individuals were given grotesque names such as 'Sir Bartholomew Baldbreech of Buttocksbury, in the County of Breakneck', whilst Lincoln's Inn had a Christmas King called Jack Straw, the name of an alleged leader of the English Rising of 1381. Again though, preferences changed, and in 1519 Jack Straw and his adherents were banned from Lincoln's Inn.[22]

There were sometimes points when the abstract or symbolic transgression of misrule was equated with or directed at real people and situations, either on festival occasions or at other times. Some of the views of misrule considered in chapter 1 give the impression that misrule was on the whole progressive and democratic in its impulse, and that its victims generally had it coming. The alleged effects of watching Robin Hood plays, probably written by Sir Richard Morison and communicated to Henry VIII sometime after the dissolution of the monasteries, might be seen in this light: '[i]n somer comenly upon the holy daies in most places of your realm, ther be playes of Robyn hoode, mayde Marian, freer Tuck, wherin besides the lewdenes and rebawdry that ther is opened to the people, disobedience also to your officers, is tought, whilest these good bloodes go about to take from the shiref of Notyngham one that for offendyng the lawes shulde have suffered execution.'[23] Here the implication is that those who watch such plays, and perhaps also the performers themselves, might seek to emulate such disrespect for royal authority outside of the play. This example in isolation tends to bear out the idea that the politics of misrule were a continuation of class warfare by other means.

That said, misrule could target the marginal as well as the powerful, sometimes with derogatory language and earthy symbolism, but at other times with murderous intent and deadly consequences. After foreign craftsmen and merchants and their property were attacked in London on 'Evil May Day' in 1517 a number of apprentices and their ringleaders were put to death, and the future observance of May Day was curtailed. The allegation was that under the cover of the events of May Day, the apprentices had planned an assault on foreigners in the city: the apprentices were to gather together in large numbers in the fields, and then return to the city with the leafy branches used to decorate houses in order to avoid any suspicion.[24] This was not the only occasion when festive celebrations were used to disguise violent intent: both Henry IV and Henry V survived plots to have them assassinated while they were watching a mumming.[25] In considering examples like these, it needs to be remembered that misrule was just one of a number of practices used for more aggressive purposes in medieval England: there was no judicial monopoly on violence or retribution. For instance, in his discussion of unlawful hunting in England between 1485 and 1640, Roger Manning has shown that as well as conventional poaching there were also cases of what are termed 'general huntings', which were 'a kind of skimmington by which the local community attempted to punish possessors of game reserves for outrageous behaviour'.[26] To sum up, misrule did not take place in some autonomous festive sphere removed from the concerns of everyday life: in common with other activities like hunting and outdoor sports in the Middle Ages, it was sometimes implicated in concerns far removed from its ostensible purpose. The self-conscious sense of transgression on which it depended may have made it more susceptible to such uses.

Finally, it is also important to recognise that features of misrule could also appear outside of what we would consider to be their usual festival context. This was especially the case with political and social upheavals or confrontations such as riots or revolts, when imagery or forms of organisation from popular customs might well find their way into events. For instance, in an important article Thomas Pettitt has explored the interaction of seasonal festivity and social revolt in England. He refers to work by Yves-Marie Bercé on popular revolts to try to explain why elements that are normally associated with festivity are present in incidents ranging from the English Rising of 1381 to the Bristol bridge riots of the eighteenth century:

> On the one hand ... the misrule attendant on seasonal festival can boil over to produce serious social upheaval ... On the other hand there is a converse, and potentially more significant, relationship: the 'apparatus' of festivity, Bercé suggests, can detach itself from its specific seasonal context and acquire a function in revolt or unrest at other times, triggered by other factors.

So Pettitt's suggestion is that aspects of misrule, such as the groups into which people were organised, or the disguises or language that they used on festive occasions, could sometimes appear outside of their usual calendar occasion, in order to make a particular protest or rebellion more effective.[27] In the next chapter an example of this transferral in examined, in a case where a group of Norwich citizens put on a Shrovetide procession in January as a way of making a particular point about local issues.

This brief examination of the range of contexts in which we find misrule in the medieval period has shown something of the breadth of its possible functions. In relation to our example from St Mary at Hill, we can try to place hocking within this variety of meanings. In fact, despite all the talk of radicalism or revolutionary intent that we encountered in the previous chapter, there is no reason why hocking in St Mary at Hill should not have been carried out in a perfectly orthodox and middle-of-the-road manner most of the time. The elements of reversal which hocking employed, namely the ability to tie people up and demand ransom money from them, especially women towards men, could well have formed a risqué but respectable means of raising money for church funds in this case. Everyone has the potential to reverse or mix up their established ways of behaving, and to do so can be a sign of one's appreciation of a shared culture, as much as it can also be a way of opposing those constraints. Our language is necessarily tentative here, since there is no way of being absolutely sure about the tone of this occasion, given the information in the sources. That said, by considering the range of possible meanings that misrule can have, we can narrow down the particular sense of this example or any other, prior to a closer analysis.

The politics of carnival

In this final section our aim is to see how, having narrowed down the likely range of meanings, we can now begin to explore them in more detail. The aim is to get away from an approach which sees misrule as a static or closed cycle which always achieves particular results, and develop a more subtle and sensitive method for analysing its meanings, both planned and unforseen. There is nothing worse than telling a joke and finding that your audience doesn't laugh, and as we saw earlier, we need to be attuned to the unexpected in thinking about the social meanings of misrule, building these principles into our analysis. As festive misrule is a genre which mixes up expectations it is particularly susceptible to (or even embraces) the vagaries of chance – this is clearly part of its attraction for some people, as well as part of its fear for others! Here we can focus more fully on the question of 'the politics of carnival'.

One of the many problems with the safety-valve view of misrule is that it tends to reduce the variety and dynamism of these customs to something predictable and rather boring. Part of the reasoning behind this view is that as we don't generally find evidence for social changes following performances of misrule, they can't have played a role in the kinds of shifts in power or status that we know were taking place in the Middle Ages. This is, for example, what MacLean implies when she writes that although Hocktide may provide some evidence for the contestation of power between the sexes, it does not actually seem to have been an agent of social change.[28] The problem with this kind of interpretation is that it assumes a rather unrealistic link between intentions and activities, which can be illustrated by considering a modern analogy. Suppose a woman runs a marathon in England dressed as a fox. We can assume that this is not her everyday attire, but what meanings does it have? This woman may be dressing up for fun, or she may be doing it to protest about the hunting of wild animals for sport. If a law banning fox-hunting is not passed in parliament the next day, does this mean that she has failed in her aims? Obviously not, because we have jumped to unrealistic conclusions about her intentions, and the causes and effects of her actions. Even if it does turn out that she was dressing up to make a protest, we would not expect overnight success; rather, we might say that the stunt had raised public consciousness of hunting as an issue, perhaps leading to further support for the anti-hunt lobby, and so on: movements for change take time to work.

A similar point can be made about festive misrule, that surely the reason why we do not have evidence for drastic social changes following these customs is because they only temporarily dramatise an altered set of social relations, and are not a concerted attempt to actually put such relations into practice. As Nicholas Davis has pointed out, 'social changes toyed with "in play" were often too thorough-going to be assimilated into everyday life'.[29] It is certainly possible that in one year the wives of the parish of St Mary at Hill, having bound, gagged and to all intents and purposes robbed a particularly loathsome local man, may have wished their actions to have had a more permanent effect. However, there is a great deal of difference between a money-raising exercise and a determined attempt to achieve universal female emancipation by tying men up and ransoming them, and so it makes little sense to judge the former in terms of the aims of the latter, or imagine that revolt and reversal are one and same thing. This principle is true for misrule more generally: the inverted state of affairs that constitutes the heart of the custom does not necessarily express a dissatisfaction with the wider social situation, although it could well do. Such a link must be demonstrated, not assumed.

In thinking about these possibilities, it is clear that the emphasis must be on studying the effects rather than the intentions of misrule. Of course all customs were carried out by people who had particular ideas of what they wanted to achieve, and we certainly need to be aware of these aims and motivations. That said, focusing too much on intentions tends to encourage us to judge the material in terms of the immediate success or failure of individual performances, and demands that we know what the original purpose was. This can often be difficult to decide when we have participants of different ages or of varying status, and when the kinds of records that survive are unlikely to record all the details that would help to inform our judgements. By contrast, if we think about the effects and outcomes of a performance, we can adopt a wider perspective and take into account a variety of meanings, including the unexpected and the unplanned, as well as the consequences over the longer term.

To take some examples, the meaning of a traditional custom can be changed by the context in which it is performed, so that what are ostensibly the same set of actions may acquire a new significance in different years. Misrule can be especially prone to this effect since it tends to dramatise situations that are based around points of potential conflict, such as gender, property or hierarchy. For instance as regards the gathering of foliage and wood at midsummer, such a practice might often be performed in a relatively mundane way, where the branches needed to decorate houses or for bonfires are procured without causing too much damage to the land of a local lord. Alternatively, given the emergence of local grievances and a desire to make a point, the custom could be used to make a land-owner pay a heavy price in terms of lost and damaged resources: whole areas of woodland might be hacked down and carried off (such an example will be discussed further in chapter 4). In certain circumstances therefore, misrule could have worked to increase resolve or antagonism about contentious issues, rather than necessarily dissipating them as the safety-valve model would suggest. This certainly seems to have been one of the fears which Sir Richard Morison had about Robin Hood plays for example, since he alleged that disobedience to the present king's officers was being taught in the dramatisation of this tale.

We can also think about meanings which are less a consequence of the actual imagery or actions of the performance itself, and have more to do with factors outside of the festive context. In relation to the hocking at St Mary at Hill for example, we can suggest that the popularity of this custom for women might have depended upon more than just the enjoyment afforded by the chance to tie up a few of the local youths for the day; it may have also provided women with a chance to offset some of the social and economic changes of the period. That is, while women in general were facing a squeeze in their employment prospects in the late fifteenth century, the popularity of hocking at this time can be seen as reflecting the opportunities which it gave then to raise money for their parish church, and thereby enjoying a greater respectability than would otherwise have been possible.[30] The meanings of hocking were not therefore limited to the way that the custom divided up protagonists and victims by sex, but may also be explored in relation to the wider social context in which the custom took place.

Of course, one difficulty we face is that many of the meanings that misrule could potentially carry are unlikely to have been recorded in surviving historical documents. In fact one of the useful qualities of misrule in the Middle Ages was the way that its participants could make statements in a medium where it might go unnoticed (the 'hidden transcript'), or else adapt a performance in order to drop in topical allusions and comments.[31] As Anthony Gash has argued in his paper on 'Carnival against Lent', a festive morality play like *Mankind* had transgressive potential, in the sense that the actors could exploit the text's ambiguities in order to articulate social and political grievances, depending upon the nature of their audience. Gash stresses that the political meanings of these texts would have been generated *in performance*, and depended upon the active participation of the audience.[32] Although there is no evidence that *Mankind* was performed in this way, evidence from sixteenth-century sources does support the notion that dissident political sentiments could be expressed through festive drama. Sandra Billington has cited a number of cases, including the well-known incident at certain May games in Suffolk in 1537, where an actor playing Husbandry 'said many things against gentlemen more than was in the book of the play.'[33] In the end, however, the full extent to which misrule was accompanied by subtle allusions or more overt references to topical events in medieval England is something which can only be guessed at.

The irony here is that the more effective the concealed allusion, the less likely it is that we as researchers are going to know about it. This absence of evidence makes it difficult to judge how far misrule did act as a medium for political meanings in medieval England. This relates to a wider point, that the relative invisibility of popular politics is often a reflection of deliberate caution, what Scott calls 'a tactical choice born of a prudent awareness of the balance of power', rather than an indication of political quiescence.[34] Even where it is clear that direct action was taken on occasions of misrule, this must always be carefully analysed in order to determine its political priorities. For instance, Steve Rappaport has suggested that 'the disorderly behaviour of young men in sixteenth-century London was hardly ever organised or purposeful, at least not consciously' on occasions like Shrovetide.[35] Surely though, we would need to investigate the tactical considerations which shaped these kinds of brief and what look on the surface like unplanned public actions, instead of seeing them as just the functional venting of youthful male frustration: in fact the most 'successful' kind of direct action is that which deliberately explodes for a brief moment, and then allows its perpetrators to slip away. In the light of these observations, the most productive kind of investigation of the dynamics of festive misrule will look as closely as possible at the available evidence, with an awareness of the different ways in which social and political grievances can be articulated.

In some instances, however, a political dimension will be clear from the start, and in such cases it is important to get our terminology right. Peter Burke's discussion of the likely functions of Carnival has emphasised the limitations of the safety-valve model, since in the early modern period there were some serious riots and disturbances on festival occasions, and political grievances were given clear expression. That said, if these occasions are just seen in terms of an exceptional explosion of an otherwise contained class antagonism, this would be to accept for the most part the terms of the safety-valve model, and its resultant problems. A better approach is to reconsider what these exceptional incidents properly represent. First, it is important to clarify the different parties who were involved, since the language of the safety-valve model has in the past tended to represent them in terms of opposing class enemies, whereas a closer examination can show a diversity of participants and alliances. Second, these incidents must not be considered in isolation, as if the festival occasion was somehow the only vehicle other than outright revolt through which medieval people took action to change their social and political circumstances. It is important to see these actions in the context of a larger strategy or campaign that can be traced in the sources. For example, in Coventry in the later fifteenth-century, the hacking-down of large amounts of foliage during the summer can be placed alongside other forms of action such as attempts to have legislation properly observed, negotiations, confrontations, the posting of broadsides, and appeals to the members of the royal court, to cite just a selection from the methods that were employed in the disputes over land use in the town at this period.[36] Direct action on occasions of misrule will almost certainly form part of a wider situation, whose terms of reference are vital to the overall analysis.

Third, and most importantly, we can adopt a more constructive language for discussing the dynamics of the interplay between the various agents in cases of politicised misrule, and their resulting outcomes. For such a vocabulary it is useful to look to other instances where this sort of issue has been debated. In the secondary literature on early modern English drama, for example, there has been considerable discussion of the extent to which the apparently subversive elements in these plays actually worked to secure the power of the state, the suggestion being that their subversion was produced and permitted so that it could be all the more effectively contained.[37] This issue has obvious similarities with the safety-valve model of misrule that has been examined in this book. In a suggestive article Theodore Leinwand has reviewed the debate and has put forward a more productive model for thinking about how the different sectors of society interact to bring about social change. Noting that the debate has been framed in terms of either subversion or containment, as either one or the other being successful, Leinwand goes on to argue:

> Perhaps we can reconceive the binarisms of social process as other than conflict leading to one-sided victory. Compromise, negotiation, exchange, accommodation, give and take – these bases for social relations and change are as recognizable as those mentioned thus far ... I believe that a model based on negotiation and exchange may prove useful where now familiar paradigms seem unsatisfactory. In particular I want to attribute change to something other than subversion ... Unlike subversion, negotiated change is dependent on the agency of two or more parties that are not entirely content with the status quo. A model of change that makes room for negotiation acknowledges the persistence of coercive discipline but argues that disciplines themselves, not only the forces resisting them, may be eroded or curbed.[38]

Such a model has clear advantages for discussing how occasions of politicised misrule were able to contribute to attempts to bring about change. That is, when direct action was taken on festival occasions, they enabled particular aspects of social relations to be contested, such as the ability of individuals to take the initiative to correct perceived infringements of their liberties. Rather than inflicting terminal damage upon the ruling class, such actions were able to prompt negotiations or force local concessions which, when considered as part of wider strategy, could prove effective in achieving specific aims and goals.

Conclusion

The aim of this chapter has been to offer a guide to the effective investigation and interpretation of the sources, by means of a more secure definition of what misrule was, and a full discussion of how we go about finding out what it did. Throughout the chapter, reference has been made to medieval examples in support of the arguments, both from the published work of other scholars and from my own case-studies. What remains to be done therefore is for the benefits of this method to be demonstrated in more concrete terms, and this will be accomplished through two case-studies, each of which sheds new light on a relatively well-known incident of misrule from fifteenth-century England. It is helpful to explain in brief the rationale behind the choice of these studies, and the pitfalls that they present. The first part of this book has shown how festive misrule can be used as a general term for an eclectic range of customs which none the less shared a common feature in their use of inversions and reversals. These customs could have a variety of outcomes and meanings, from middle of the road to outright bawdiness and even murderous intent. The problem we face in interpreting the evidence is that the surviving records do not reflect in equal measure all these meanings: they inevitably focus on situations which tend to get recorded, such as those where money was collected, or which led to a court case and litigation. As already suggested, this means that we have to think carefully about what the evidence is telling us. It also means that the richer veins of material which enable us to look in detail at the politics of carnival tend to be high-profile cases: we don't get to know about the mummer who cursed his local lord as he trudged off home to change out of his women's apparel. The danger therefore is that our view of misrule becomes skewed towards the explosive events that made it into the historical record in the first place, and we have to keep a sense of perspective and balance.

The preceding pages have shown the variety of medieval festive misrule, and so that the closer studies which constitute the remainder of the book should be seen for what they are, demonstrative rather than representative of misrule's involvement in the politics and culture of fifteenth-century England. They show what can be done when we break out of the old dualism that has blighted the interpretation of festive misrule. There is, however, a further rationale for selecting these particular cases, and for the way that they have been treated. This book has argued that the view of festive misrule as a static, self-contained and slightly provocative set of customs is unrepresentative of the evidence, and that we should prefer instead a view that perceives it as a dynamic and interconnected practice whose tone could very enormously. Such an argument can be convincingly put in the abstract, but it can also be demonstrated through actual examples, and so each of the case-studies shows in more detail one of the key attributes of this new view of medieval festive misrule. The analysis of Gladman's riding at Norwich in 1443 in chapter 3 shows the potential mobility of festive drama, and considers why a Shrovetide procession took place outside of its usual calendar occurrence, while chapter 4 considers how the custom of gathering greenery at midsummer came to form one part of a wider oppositional campaign in late medieval Coventry. To sum up, part of the problem of interpreting festive misrule for students and researchers alike has been the feeling that we should defer to what the theorists say should happen, rather than seeing for ourselves what actually did happen. This is not to say that all theorising is wrong, but at the very least it should tell us about how it arrived at its conclusions, and how we too can put its insights into practice. By providing constructive and accessible interpretations of the evidence in the second part of this book, the aim is to underline the usefulness of its new approach, both in conceptual and in methodological terms.

Notes

1 See chapter 1, 'Points of contact between anthropological and theatrical thought', in Schechner, *Between Theater and Anthropology*.

2 See chapter 3, 'Rituals of rebellion in south-east Africa', in Gluckman, *Order and Rebellion*. For a critical perspective on Gluckman's work see Norbeck, 'African rituals of conflict', Rigby, 'Some Gogo rituals of "purification"' and Babcock, 'Introduction', pp. 22–4.

3 Phythian-Adams, *Local History and Folklore*, pp. 12–30 and 31–5.

4 Twycross, 'Some approaches to dramatic festivity', pp. 6 and 17.

5 Twycross, 'Some approaches to dramatic festivity', pp. 20–6 (p. 24).

6 Babcock, 'Introduction', p. 14.

7 Stallybrass and White, *Politics and Poetics of Transgression*, pp. 23–5.

8 Stallybrass and White, *Politics and Poetics of Transgression*, pp. 17–18.

9 See Butler, 'Further reflections', p. 14. This article won an award for bad writing, but in fact it states very concisely how forms of culture have meaning over time.

10 See Pettitt, 'Protesting inversions', for a very full discussion of charivari.

11 See Mellinkoff, 'Riding backwards', for a fuller discussion of the historical uses of this device. I am grateful to Christa Grössinger for drawing my attention to this article.

12 This episode is recorded in YCA, House Book 13, fols 58–64, and is edited in *York Civic Records 4*, ed. Raine, pp. 7–13.

13 Hutton, *Rise and Fall of Merry England*, p. 9.

14 *Medieval Records of St. Mary at Hill*, ed. Littlehales, p. 230.

15 This edition is based upon a bound collection of the church's medieval records. See the introduction for more information.

16 *Medieval Records of St. Mary at Hill*, ed. Littlehales, pp. 221 and 228.

17 Somerset, 'New Historicism: old history writ large?', p. 254.

18 Burgess, 'Shaping the parish' and Jeffery, *The Parish Church of St. Mary-at-Hill*.

19 See, for example, Randall, *Images in the Margins of Gothic Manuscripts* and Grössinger, *The World Upside-Down: English Misericords*.

20 Duffy, *Stripping of the Altars*, pp. 13–4.

21 Hutton, *Stations of the Sun*, pp. 99–100.

22 Horner, 'Christmas at the Inns of Court', pp. 45–6.

23 Anglo, 'An early Tudor programme', p. 179.

24 Vergil, *Anglica Historia*, ed. Hay, pp. 242–7; Stow, *Survey of London*, ed. Kingsford, 1, p. 99.

25 Lancashire, *Dramatic Texts and Records*, pp. 129 and 285.

26 Manning, *Hunters and Poachers*, p. 2.

27 Pettitt, '"Here comes I, Jack Straw"', pp. 3 and 6.

28 MacLean, 'Hocktide: a reassessment', p. 239.

29 Davis, 'The playing of miracles in England', p. 27.

30 Humphrey, 'Dynamics of urban festal culture', pp. 157–61.

31 The idea of the hidden transcript is discussed by Scott in *Domination and the Arts of Resistance*. For the application of these ideas to dramatic activity see Max Harris, *Festivals of Aztecs, Moors, and Christians*.

32 Gash, 'Carnival against Lent', pp. 94–6. For a discussion of audience responses to Tudor drama see White, 'Politics, topical meaning, and English theater audiences'.

33 Billington, *Mock Kings in Medieval Society and Renaissance Drama*, pp. 218–19 (p. 218).

34 Scott, *Domination and the Arts of Resistance*, p. 183.

35 Rappaport, *Worlds Within Worlds*, p. 11. I am grateful to Christian Liddy for bringing this reference to my attention.

36 See chapter 4.

37 Kastan and Stallybrass, 'Introduction', pp. 5–7.

38 Leinwand, 'Negotiation and New Historicism', pp. 479–80.

3

Seasonal drama and local politics in Norwich, 1443

It would be fair to say that the citizens of present-day Norwich are not on the whole thought of as troublesome revolutionaries. It can therefore be somewhat difficult to believe that their medieval forebears enjoyed a reputation as some of the most lawless troublemakers in the reign of Henry VI, but this is indeed how they were portrayed in several contemporary chronicles.[1] One particular incident which did much to contribute to this reputation has become known to historians as 'Gladman's Insurrection'.[2] There are two main accounts of what happened, both of which agree on the major details of date and who was involved: on Tuesday 22 January 1443 one John Gladman, on horseback, led a procession through the streets of Norwich, at a time when the city was locked in a bitter dispute with Holy Trinity Priory over its rights to some local grain mills. However, the accounts differ greatly in the finer details of what the riding is supposed to have represented. In one version of events, recorded at an inquiry at Thetford into the incident just over a month later, it was alleged that the mayor and citizens, planning an insurrection, 'then and there arranged for John Gladman of the said city, merchant, to ride in the city on a horse, like a crowned king, with a sceptre and sword carried before him'. Furthermore, a number of others rode on horseback before him, 'with a crown upon their arms and carrying bows and arrows, as if they were valets of the crown of the lord king'; he is also alleged to have had a hundred more people following on horseback and on foot behind. 'They went around urging people in the city to come together and to make an insurrection and riots there.'[3]

A second version of these events, written in the city's records, gives a rather different impression of the incident. The account appears in a number of drafts of a document which details the wrongs done to the mayor and citizens of Norwich by two henchmen of the earl of Suffolk, Sir Thomas Tuddenham and John Heydon, who were notorious in this region for their violent and bullying conduct.[4] The fact that these two men are explicitly named suggests that the document dates from 1450 or after, when Suffolk was dead and his followers were under investigation.[5] Amongst a list of other complaints the city looked back to the inquest at Thetford on 28 February 1443, and alleged that at Tuddenham and Heydon, 'fynddyng nither conceitis no maner mater of trought wher of thei myght cause the sayd mayre and comonalte ther to be indityd, ymagined thus as insueth':

> Wher that it was so that one John Gladman of Norwich, wych was ever and at this oure is a man of sadde dispocicion and trew and faythfull to god and to the kynge, of disport as is and hever hath bene acustomyd in ony cite or borought thorought all thys reame on Fastyngonge Tuesdaye, ¹in the ende of Crystemasse and by fore Condelmesse¹ mad a disporte wyght his neyburghs, hawyng his hors trappyd with tynne foyle and other nyse disgysy thynggis corowned as kyng of Cristmesse in token that all myrth that seson shuld ende, with the xii monthes of the yer afore hym dysguysyd after the seson there of requiryth, and Lenton clad in white with redheryngys skynnys and his hors trappyd with oyster shells after him, in token that sadnesse schuld folowyn and an holy tyme. And so rod in diverse stretes of the cite with othr peple with hym dysguysyd makyng myrth, disportes and pleyes. The sayd Sir Thomas and John Heydon among many othr ful straunge and untrewe presentements made by perjery of the sayd inquest caused the sayd mayr and comonalte and the sayd John Gladman to be indityd of that, that ther shuld an ymagined to a mad a comoun risyng and a corouned the sayd John Gladman as kynge with coroun, septure

and diademe, wher thai never ment it ne never swich a thynge ymagined as in the sayd presentement it shewyth more playn.[6]

The city were therefore arguing that a procession that was customary to Shrove Tuesday ('Fastyngonge Tuesdaye') had been presented to the jury at Thetford as a common rising, an attempt to set up a new king against the existing monarch and incite rebellion. We may note that the issue of why a procession which was customary to Shrovetide was put on at this time, five weeks prior to Shrove Tuesday in that year, is carefully avoided. Although the city suggests that such a riding was something common in towns and cities at Shrovetide, in fact it is fairly unique in England, and on the whole there is very little evidence for any major public celebrations prior to the beginning of Lent in England, in comparison with the continent.[7] It is likely that for religious reasons, and possibly for reasons of inclement weather, the festival of Shrovetide/Carnival did not develop in England in the same way in which it developed in other parts of Europe in the Middle Ages.[8]

Who was John Gladman? Whatever their other differences, both accounts of this event do name Gladman as the principal character. Unfortunately very little is known about him, except that he was a Norwich merchant and a member of the Guild of St George. This was a powerful fraternity to which many wealthy citizens and influential local characters belonged, and its members included the earl of Suffolk, Tuddenham, Heydon and Thomas Wetherby, the latter being the principal leader of the faction within the city which enjoyed the patronage of Suffolk.[9] So we are not dealing here with implacable class enemies, but with rival groups amongst the elite of the town and their supporters: this is as much about personalities as it is public politics, although it can be difficult to ascribe motives to particular individuals given the evidence that we have.[10] What we do know is that each account differs in what it says happened, and more importantly, in what the implications of its representation were. The main point of contention is what Gladman's act of dressing up as a king represents: both accounts see it as transgressive, but each offers a different account of what such an action means, by placing the performance in a wider context.

In the account given at Thetford, the suggestion is that the king-figure and the riding represented an attempt to set up a new king and start an insurrection in the city. This of itself was a treasonable act, but it might seem difficult to have convinced a jury that a upstart merchant from Norwich should realistically fancy himself as the next monarch. However, such an allegation may have carried more credibility in uncertain times: concern was being expressed about the king's judgement in the early 1440s, while the earl of Suffolk's machinations made East Anglia a tense and dangerous place at this period.[11] So the terms in which the riding was represented were picking up on present fears, and they made sure that they included descriptions of all the accoutrements of kingship like sceptre, sword and armed supporters. The city's defence of what happened by contrast takes an alternative tack. The passage admits that a king was represented, but argues that he was a mock king who was part of a Shrovetide celebration, and therefore relatively harmless, intent on making 'myrth, disportes and pleyes' rather than usurping the present ruler. As all those involved were taking part in such a festive event, they have been gravely misrepresented by their accusers, who have wilfully misunderstood the purpose of what took place. The existence of the several different drafts of this presentment in the Norwich archives reinforces the impression that the city was seeking to put the best light on what had happened: another draft of the same passage has Gladman's horse 'trappid with smale bledders, puddyngs and lynks', a phrase which has then been crossed out in favour of the more prosaic tin foil.[12] Apparently the city preferred to say it with fish (in Lent's costume) rather than saying it with meat, to adapt Ladurie's observations about continental carnival imagery, thereby avoiding the connotations of butchery and slaughter which meat might carry at this season.[13]

Our immediate reaction when reading these differing accounts is to think about which version was the right one: who was telling the truth, and who was embellishing their story for best effect? On the face of it we might have a case of some innocent revellers being falsely accused, but then why were they taking part in a Shrovetide procession in January, five weeks ahead of the proper date of the feast? If Gladman and his associates were just riding for fun, why should anyone want to portray them as rebels and revolutionaries? And most importantly for the study of misrule, what meanings did this particular performance have for those who watched it and took part? Although several scholars have already examined this incident in some detail, and many more have referred to it in passing, a new understanding of these events can be offered, which makes use of the new methodology outlined in chapter 2.[14] There are two stages to our analysis: first, we can establish the wider course of events in which Gladman's riding took place, using the sources mentioned already and additional evidence that helps to shed light on this case, such as the city's Liber Albus or White Book, in which civic business is recorded. Second, we can look more closely at the riding itself, to discern its meanings and to consider its influence and impact on local events.

A troubled city: Norwich in 1443

We can begin our analysis by looking more closely at the immediate situation in Norwich and indeed in England and the continent in the early part of the fifteenth century. At this time the English were fighting to defend their territories in France, with the famous Joan of Arc rallying the French in 1429, the same year that the youthful Henry VI was crowned. By the early 1440s there were suspicions about Henry's ability to govern, and various factions vied for power and patronage. In this climate the earl of Suffolk, William de la Pole, became one of the king's most influential advisers: he enjoyed immense power, especially in East Anglia. As mentioned earlier, two of his cronies were Sir Thomas Tuddenham and John Heydon, who did much of his dirty work, and they were accused of being behind the insurrection case brought against the mayor and citizens of Norwich in 1443. In fact, on the whole, Suffolk and his followers appear to have sided with the prior of the cathedral priory of Norwich and disaffected former office-holders like the twice mayor Thomas Wetherby, in the bitter factional disputes which dogged the city in the 1430s and 1440s.[15] The particular dispute that interests us is the long-running battle between the city and the priory about who had jurisdiction over certain areas of the city, and the claim from the abbot of St Benet's Hulme that the city's newly-built mills on the River Wensum, which were only a decade or so old at this date, interfered with the mills on his manor. By October 1441 the city's governors had reached the point where they had agreed to submit to the arbitration of the earl of Suffolk, in order to reach a settlement on these matters. The retrospective account in the city's Liber Albus claimed the new mills had been built to replace four 'ancient' mills: 'for by cause the seid auncenne mylles stodyn longe decayede in somuche that it hadde be leke to be a desolacion if the cite hadde not the newe mylles by good dysspo[s]yd peopyll'.[16] While the jurisdictional matters were clearly of importance to the city, the people of Norwich faced a more immediate problem in that any threat to the new mills was also a threat to their food supply. The earl's verdict was issued in June 1442, and unsurprisingly it found in favour of the priory: one of the demands was that the calamitous decision that the city's mills should be taken down before 30 April next. As well as entering into bonds of £50 with the prior and bishop, the mayor, sheriffs and commonalty were also to be bound £100 to oblige them to observe all decisions made about matters between them and the abbot.[17] According to the Liber Albus, when this verdict was read to the citizens 'they under stode by the [a]warde that they shulde loos the myllys whyche shuld be an utter desolacion for the cyte and shulde cause the pepyll to goo owte of the cyte'.[18]

Understandably, the mayor and his officers were reluctant to put the city's seal to any documents which threatened such adverse consequences, and various legal counters to the award were attempted.[19] However, matters appear to have been forced to a head in the latter part of January 1443. For an account of these events, which included Gladman's riding, a city assembly where the common seal was borne away, and the 'siege' of Holy Trinity Priory, we have three main sources of information. First, there are the two indictments which were taken at the inquest at Thetford on 28 February 1443, one of which has already been mentioned. Second, there is the city's defence of Gladman's riding which occurs in the presentments made against Wetherby's faction, thought to have been written *c.* 1450, also mentioned above. Third, there is the retrospective account in the city's Liber Albus, which recalls these events from the perspective of 1482.[20] While all of these documents are selective in the information which they relate and what they leave out, something of an overall picture can be pieced together from them.

According to the Liber Albus account, Wetherby's supporters and the abbot pressurised the city into calling an assembly at which the bond could be sealed:

> And after this for the dylyvere of the [a]warde anno xxi[mo] [of the reign of Henry VI] grett labours were made be the seid Wederby and hys adherentes and the councell of the seid abbotts to have hadde the seid obligacon of an £100 under the comon seall of the cite, and the comones wold never agree. And so after warde in the day of the convercion of Seynt Poule anno xxi[mo] h vi[ti] [25 January 1443], the seid Thomas Wederby and the abbott's councell and others that they cowde gette over to them come to Norwich and caused on William Hempsted that tyme beyng maire to sette a semble, and so he dede.[21]

This account, written almost forty years after the event, reads as if the assembly was called immediately, but we might expect that some advance notice would have been necessary in order to organise affairs. The city's rules recommended that assemblies be called on holy days, when there were no markets in the city, for the convenience of merchants; although this guidance was not always adhered to, a matter of this magnitude would have clearly required a full turnout, and so 25 January, the Conversion of St Paul, would have been a likely date for a meeting after Christmas.[22] Thus the citizens who, according to the Liber Albus, had 'seid that the abbott shude never have there obligacion under ther comon seall in distruccion of the kyng's cite to performe that a warde', were faced with the prospect of a common assembly where exactly that was to be done.[23] It is in this context that on Tuesday 22 January, three days before this critical city assembly, that Gladman's riding appears to have taken place. There has been some uncertainty in the past about the actual date of the riding, with the phrase 'on Fastyngonge Tuesdaye' being interpreted as the specific day on which it took place. However, we should really envisage a comma after this phrase, so that the city were only claiming that Gladman had ridden in a procession that was *customary* to Shrovetide, rather than on that day itself. This interpretation is borne out by the fact that the draft reproduced above includes the interlineated phrase 'in the ende of Crystemasse and by fore Condelmesse' to refer to the actual time of year that the riding happened. In addition, the account given at the inquiry at Thetford clearly states that it was on Tuesday 22 January 1443 that the riding took place.

The significance of Gladman's riding and the problem of the two rather different accounts of it will be discussed in more detail below. First though, it is important to have some idea of the events which followed, in order to understand the relationship of the riding to them. We continue from where we left off in the Liber Albus with the mayor, William Hempsted, having called an assembly on Friday 25 January:

> [The] which semble hewlde from [no time is given] of the cloke tyll v after and grete importunes labours made to have hadde the obligacion sealed under the comon seale, the comons of the cite gaddred them to geder in a grett nomber and come to the halle and token a wey the common seall to that entent that the obligacion shulde nat be a sealyd.[24]

Also on this day, the indictments taken at Thetford allege (so presumably after the assembly), the mayor, commonalty and three thousand others gathered in the city, summoned by the ringing of various bells. Shouting about their intentions with the none-too-subtle cry of 'Let us burn the priory, and kill the prior and monks', they laid siege to the priory until four o'clock on the following afternoon, when the monks handed over certain evidence concerning an indenture made in 1429.[25] This document had been sealed in order to resolve an earlier juris-dictional dispute between the city and the priory, although its outcome had been to the priory's advantage. Philippa Maddern has argued that the Thetford account of a violent 'siege' of the priory is not borne out in the surviving evidence; the only known damage done was to the priory's prison and stocks, and the besiegers even had to kidnap a neighbouring gentlemen and threaten him with defenestration in order to have a gun aimed at the priory walls.[26] Still, these disturbances were sufficient grounds for the abbot of St Benet's and Wetherby to accuse the mayor and citizens of riot and insurrection; they 'made a subgestyon to the kyng and hys councell ageynste the seid maire and many others that they werre rysers ageynst the kyng'.[27]

Consequently, an inquiry was established on 11 February in order to make enquiries into the lack of good government by the mayor, sheriffs and aldermen of Norwich.[28] In addition, the mayor and other citizens were summoned to Westminster, and after his appearance there on 13 February the mayor William Hempsted was fined £50 and committed to the Fleet prison, where he remained until 26 March.[29] As we have already seen, an inquest took place at Thetford on 28 February, at which the accusation was that Gladman had ridden through the town like a crowned king; this inquest was adjourned, and it was at a further hearing at Norwich on 4 March that the city's attorney abandoned its plea, allegedly due to the influence of Thomas Wetherby. At a final inquest at Thetford on 14 March it was judged that the liberties and franchises of the city should be seized; they were not restored until November 1447, after a payment of one thousand marks.[30] This course of events can be followed in the minutes of the meetings of the Privy Council, where the king asked for a search of the Exchequer's records in order to see how the franchises of the city had been seized on a previous occasion: it was only as recently as 1437 that the people of Norwich had lost their right to manage their own affairs for a time. Preparations were also made for John Clifton to become governor of the town in another such eventuality.[31] With the mayor of Norwich absent, 'Thomas Wedyrby and his adherentys in the mene tyme toke upon them to be rewlers of the cite', and made the most of their advantage. On 10 March, they took the city's seal from the common chest and sealed obligations to the abbot of St Benet's and to the prior and to the bishop of Norwich, although the bond between the mayor and aldermen and the abbot was later proved to be illegal, since the mayor had been in prison when it had been sealed.[32] The contested mills were also damaged to such an extent that the town's bakers were forced to use mills ten miles away from the city for a time.[33]

Gladman's riding

Previous scholarly discussions of Gladman's riding have tended to take the line that the two different accounts of the incident are mutually exclusive; in some cases, an explanation has been put forward for which of them is to be preferred, whilst in others, only one of the versions has been cited. Norman Tanner for example suggests that the Thetford indictment 'seems nearer the truth than the city government's version for several reasons', including the fact that 'the city government offered no explanation why a "disport" such as was customary on Shrove Tuesday took place more than a month earlier'.[34] Philippa Maddern has taken the view that in the document of *c.* 1450 the citizens were trying to pass Gladman's riding off as a harmless Shrove Tuesday procession, when in fact it had been martial in character and associated with the events of 25 January:

> Their whole endeavour was to prove it innocent, rather than riotous, by alleging that it was part of the customary 'merth and disporte and pleyes' of Shrovetide … This was a lie; January 25 fell a good five weeks before Shrove Tuesday in 1443. We must therefore assume that the city hoped, by these means, to palliate an undeniable truth.[35]

Maddern's reasoning is that as Shrove Tuesday was at least five weeks away (on 5 March), the procession could not possibly have been part of the celebrations associated with Shrovetide.[36] Hence, in the absence of any explanation for why a Shrovetide procession might have occurred in January, the Shrovetide link is perceived to be a cover story designed to exonerate the city, leaving the Thetford indictment to become the 'truth' of what actually took place. A more overtly martial procession may also help to explain the disturbances which were to follow on Friday 25 January and over the weekend. One difficulty with this line of reasoning is how those who wrote the *c.* 1450 passage could have hoped to pass off a misrepresentation of this magnitude, given that any recourse to the Thetford indictments would have exposed them immediately. Also, as I have already argued, one of the drafts of the city's defence contains the interlineated phrase 'in the ende of Crystemasse and by fore Condelmesse' after the mention of Shrove Tuesday. This phrase clearly rules out the idea that the city were trying to claim that the riding *took place* at Shrovetide, and instead confirms that they were only claiming that Gladman had ridden in a procession that was *customary* to Shrovetide: the date of the actual riding was at the end of the Christmas season and before Candlemas (2 February). But why should a group of citizens have chosen to have put on a Shrovetide pageant at this particular time? By thinking more carefully about the imagery of the occasion and the local situation in which the performance took place, it is possible to put forward a plausible explanation for why Gladman's riding occurred when it did.

As we have seen, Gladman's procession of the seasons took place several days prior to a crucial common assembly, at which the city's representatives were due to seal a document binding the city to carry out the earl of Suffolk's judgement to dismantle the new mills before 30 April. My suggestion is that a group of Norwich citizens chose to stage a public display of their dissatisfaction with the situation, and it is also possible that they had the intention of affecting the outcome of the forthcoming assembly. Accordingly, they drew upon and mobilised festival

73

imagery that was particularly appropriate to the situation that the city faced, thereby confronting its population with a symbolic dramatisation of their own predicament; the imagery deployed was a procession of the months headed by a representation of Christmas, presumably in a similar form to that outlined in the document of *c.* 1450. Clearly, the citizens and other people who encountered these celebrations outside of their usual calendar context would have been struck by their anomalous timing, and made to think about their purpose and what they signified. As we saw in chapter 2, Tom Pettitt has shown how festival customs were a feature of English revolts between the Middle Ages and the nineteenth century, and so this case suggests that calendar could play a part in disputes of a more local, non-revolutionary character.[37]

Gladman's riding highlighted the opposition between the end of the Christmas season and the beginning of Lent; in the procession the figure of Lent followed after the King of Christmas. This image would have had an especially topical meaning in the context of the city's disputes with a number of local ecclesiastical institutions. As Lent was a period of fasting, the personification of Lent this early in the year may have helped to focus anxieties about how the city would be supplied with food in the future, given the impending destruction of the city's mills. Furthermore, while the calendar period of Lent would come and go, questions about food supply would continue to trouble the city: Easter Sunday fell on 21 April in 1443, just over a week before the deadline for the demolition of the mills.[38] The fact that Lent was at the rear of the procession, symbolising that 'sadnesse shuld folowyn and an holy tyme', had more than just a seasonal meaning in this context; it was a symbolic expression of the city's predicament, and perhaps also an incitement to take action to forestall these consequences. This link between the symbolism of the procession and the question of food supply need not have been the only meaning that Gladman's riding could have had: given the complexity of civic affairs at this time, there are no doubt all sorts of other meanings that were drawn from this incident. However, as the choice of imagery in this situation appears to have been particularly well suited to the immediate context in which it was deployed, it offers a good explanation for why Gladman's riding may have taken the form of a procession customary to Shrovetide.

The appropriateness of its imagery was not the only tactical feature of the Shrovetide format. A further advantage which it offered was that if a defence of the incident became necessary, the participants could always argue that their actions were entirely harmless, just play and nothing else. This is in fact the defence that the Norwich citizens had recourse to some years later, stressing that Gladman's riding had involved 'makyng myrth, disportes and pleyes', rather than the insurrection that they had been accused of. This use of a particular discourse of play is also found in other cases where drama or games were involved in contentious matters. To cite two examples, at York in February 1538 one Thomas Atkinson, merchant, 'of the aige of xxvi yeres or ther abouts', and John Bean, innholder, went to the house of Sir Christopher Painter, priest and chaplain to the mayor of York, John North, between ten and eleven o'clock in the evening. Their purpose was apparently to play a practical joke on the priest by imitating the mayor's servants. Thomas confessed to saying to Painter, 'Sir Christofer, my lord mayer prays you to be with hym in the mornyng betyms for he hath strangers that cam furth of Lyncolneshier, and therfor ye muste bryng a pyke in the mornyng very tymelie about thre or iiii of the clokk, for they ryd very tymly fro my lord mayer'. Unfortunately for the hoaxers they were recognised and consequently brought before the city council to be examined. Thomas accused John of putting him up to it, but in his defence John declared that he, Thomas and six co-conspirators were 'all agreyd that the said Thomas Atkynson shuld say suche words unto the said Sir Christofer *for a sporte and pastyme and for noon other purpos*'.[39] They were all committed to ward to await punishment at the mayor's discretion; two years earlier, Mayor John North had been the target of the slanderous bills that were mentioned in chapter 2. Another example comes from Lancashire in 1536, in the context of the Pilgrimage of Grace. In this case it was alleged that one Hugh Parker and others, with 'their faces colored and disguysed and in harnes [armour]', visited various houses in Chorley around midnight in order to see if certain householders would be sworn to the commons. In his defence before the Justices of the Peace of Lancaster, Parker declared that he had met two men who had been playing games at an alehouse; he 'thoght they had gon to make pastym for he being ignorant of their ungracious purpose foloed theym *and no other thing dyd nor intended to doo but myrthe and pastyme* orels he wold not haue foloed theym in nowise'.[40]

While the defendants in these two cases were not in a position to deny their actions, they could at least hope to diminish their significance by claiming that these actions were interpreted the wrong way, having been meant only in play or jest. In the case of Gladman's riding, this is exactly the line of defence that was attempted some years later, although it is not clear whether it was actually used at the trial which followed the incident itself. The Liber Albus account suggests that Thomas Delrow, who had been appointed by Wetherby in Hempsted's absence to represent the mayor, sheriffs and commonalty, relinquished their plea at the request of Thomas Wetherby and his faction, and so we do not know what their defence would have been.[41] In the light of the defence that was put forward in the *c.* 1450 document though, it is reasonable to assume that it may have been along similar lines. To sum up then, we have seen that there are two key reasons to support the view that Gladman's riding took the form of a Shrovetide procession; first, it was an apposite comment on the city's current situation and second, it offered the participants a means of covering themselves if that proved to be necessary.

The irony of Gladman's riding is that some of the individuals who stood against the city were opponents of equal creativity and resourcefulness. At the Thetford inquest on 28 February, the riding was represented as an usurpation of royal authority, thereby framing all of the events which followed in a narrative of rebellion and insurrection. Also, according to the Liber Albus account, efforts were apparently made to have the mayor and other citizens arrested as traitors even before their appearance at Westminster on 13 February. So when one of the Norwich citizens, Benedict Jolly, was in London for the trial, he was confronted by a sergeant-at-arms, who asked him if he was from Norwich, and Jolly replied that he was. 'Than seid the serjaunt of armys that he was a traytour and a ryser ageynst the kyng and that he was one of thoo[se] for to make a newe kyng, and so he ledde hym forth to pryson.'[42] The narrative of insurrection was clearly persuasive at the time, even perhaps being one reason why the Norwich citizens abandoned their defence in March, and as we have seen, it has had an influence upon modern scholarly accounts of these events too. We have also seen the consequences that followed, which included the destruction of the city's mills, the imprisonment of the mayor and the loss of the city's liberties and franchises. In the short term then, Gladman's riding does not appear to have been very much of a 'success', if we were expecting it to have had some immediate and beneficial impact upon the city's fortunes. In the longer term however, as Philippa Maddern suggests, 'the city's policy of calculated public bravado did it no harm. Suffolk's hated award of 1442 was never properly sealed; after 1447 the city repaired the broken mills, argued their case again with the abbot of St Benet's Hulme (1481), and, after renegotiating the dispute with the priory (1517–24), finally brought it to a more favourable settlement'.[43]

Conclusion

The case of Gladman's riding has enabled us to bring the new approach outlined in chapter 2 to bear on a specific historical incident, and thereby tease out some of the meanings associated with this fascinating set of events. Clearly, our analysis has benefited from an open-minded approach which looks for evidence of motives, meanings and outcomes, rather than assuming that we already know what they are. This bears out the main proposal put forward in chapter 2, where it was suggested that as transgression is a basic cultural process which works by means of an inversion or intermingling of social categories, it is mistaken to argue that misrule is *intrinsically* political. Rather, the degree to which it offers a challenge to the status quo will always depend upon the contingent factors which give rise to and develop during a specific situation. Also, even in cases where misrule carries a political import, the effects of that meaning cannot be decided in the abstract (subversion or containment), but will again depend upon the forces at work in that situation. In the case of Gladman's riding at Norwich, we have a concrete example of how both of these dynamics were played out. First, we can see how the practice of mounting a Shrovetide pageant, rather than being something which is inherently radical because it contains a mock king, actually *became* politicised as a result of the context into which it was deliberately inserted. As such, the political significance of the pageant was the fact that its imagery was particularly apposite for the local situation at that time. The discourses of rebellion and of harmless play which have been identified may be understood as opposing ways of negotiating the meaning of Gladman's riding and the subsequent events in which it was implicated. Second, it is clear that the outcome of this performance cannot be decided in isolation from the other tactics which were employed by the citizens in January 1443, and that the resulting political gains and losses must be considered over the longer term. We can never know for sure whether or not Gladman's riding in January 1443 really made a difference to the course of events in Norwich. But a few years later, with Suffolk dead and his allies on the back foot, citizens recalling the riding of a king through the streets of their city may well have remembered a triumph rather than a defeat.

Notes

1 Maddern, *Violence and Social Order*, pp. 174–5.

2 Transcriptions of the documents which relate to this incident and its context are brought together under the heading of 'The riot called "Gladman's Insurrection"' in *Records of the City of Norwich*, ed. Hudson and Tingey, 1, pp. 338–56. References in this chapter are given to the original manuscripts and documents held at the Norwich Record Office, although where possible the corresponding transcriptions in Hudson and Tingey's volume or by other scholars have also been provided.

3 Tanner, *The Church in Late Medieval Norwich*, pp. 149–50. Tanner's translation is preferred over that of Hudson, in *Records of the City of Norwich*, ed. Hudson and Tingey, 1, pp. 340–1, whose version 'is much abbreviated and not always accurate' (Tanner, p. 151 n. 51).

4 Griffiths, *Reign of Henry VI*, p. 300.

5 These documents are dated by Hudson and Tingey as *c.* 1448, but they may form part of the preparations for the case against Tuddenham, Heydon and others which was underway in 1450: this is hinted at in *Records of the City of Norwich*, 1, p. 346 n. 1. See Storey, *End of the House of Lancaster*, pp. 218–9.

6 NRO, case 9c/2/2, 'Extract from the books of the Corporation of Norwich', ed. Johnson and *Records of the City of Norwich*, ed. Hudson and Tingey, 1, pp. 345–6. The differences between my transcription and the one given by Hudson and Tingey may be explained by the existence of a number of different drafts of the city's defence. My presentation of one of these drafts is inevitably a compromise, as I have sought to render it comprehensible by leaving out two interlineated emendations and keeping a third, which has been signalled in the text by superscript figures. In order to make the passage intelligible, I have omitted an interlineated 'a' between 'fastyngonge' and 'tuesdaye' and I have left out the interlineated phrase 'made them to indyte' between 'caused' and 'the'. Punctuation and capitalisation have been added, as they are crucial to the sense of when Gladman's riding took place.

7 See Davidson, 'Carnival, Lent and drama', pp. 123–4. A riding of the months is also mentioned in a visitation of the College of the Annunciation of St Mary at Leicester in 1525 (Thompson, *History of St. Mary in the Newarke*, p. 156). I am grateful to Charles Phythian-Adams for this reference.

8 'An examination of the regional pattern would require further investigation of the medieval origins of Carnival and a fuller survey of penance in the various regions'; Mansfield, *Humiliation of Sinners*, p. 140. See also Burke, *Popular Culture in Early Modern Europe*, p. 191, for

comments about the weather. For a fuller discussion of carnival and Shrovetide see Burke, *Popular Culture in Early Modern Europe*, pp. 178–204 and Hutton, *Stations of the Sun*, pp. 151–68.

9 Maddern, *Violence and Social Order*, p. 198 and Storey, *End of the House of Lancaster*, p. 219. The vocations and civic offices held by individuals named in this chapter are based upon evidence compiled from the Norwich records; for more details see Humphrey, 'Dynamics of urban festal culture', chapter 3.

10 Maddern, *Violence and Social Order*, p. 199.

11 Griffiths, *Reign of Henry VI*, pp. 251 and 587.

12 NRO, case 9c/3. The mention of these meats constitutes an intriguing link with continental Shrovetide, and is therefore a important exception to the general lack of evidence for this kind of practice in medieval England, in comparison with the continent.

13 Le Roy Ladurie, *Carnival*, pp. 317–18 and Muir, *Mad Blood Stirring*, p. 115.

14 The most detailed examination of this incident and its context is given by Maddern, *Violence and Social Order*, pp. 192–205. Other notable discussions include Blomefield, *History of the County of Norfolk*, 3, pp. 147–55; Storey, *End of the House of Lancaster*, pp. 220–5; Tanner, *The Church in Late Medieval Norwich*, pp. 146–52; Gash, 'Carnival against Lent', pp. 85–6; Duffy, *Stripping of the Altars*, p. 14; Hilton, *English and French Towns*, pp. 123–5.

15 McRee, 'Peacemaking and its limits', p. 854; Griffiths, *Reign of Henry VI*, pp. 585–6.

16 NRO, Liber Albus, fol. 67, *Records of the City of Norwich*, ed. Hudson and Tingey, 1, pp. 349–50 and Maddern, *Violence and Social Order*, pp. 193–4. Lilley suggests that the new mills were completed in 1429 (*Modernizing the Medieval City*, p. 24).

17 NRO, case 9c/14 and Maddern, *Violence and Social Order*, pp. 194–5.

18 NRO, Liber Albus, fol. 66ᵛ and *Records of the City of Norwich*, ed. Hudson and Tingey, 1, pp. 349–50.

19 Maddern, *Violence and Social Order*, pp. 195–6.

20 As mentioned above, one of the 1443 Thetford indictments has been translated by Tanner, *The Church in Late Medieval Norwich*, pp. 149–51, and it is also translated and summarised in *Records of the City of Norwich*, ed. Hudson and Tingey, 1, pp. 340–1. Maddern has briefly summarised both indictments (*Violence and Social Order*, pp. 196–7). Extracts from the presentments against Wetherby's faction written *c.* 1450 are given in *Records of the City of Norwich* 1, pp. 343–6, whilst the 1482 Liber Albus account is given on pp. 350–2.

21 NRO, Liber Albus, fol. 67 and *Records of the City of Norwich*, ed. Hudson and Tingey, 1, pp. 350–1.

22 Chapter 45, in *Records of the City of Norwich*, ed. Hudson and Tingey, 1, pp. 191–2.

23 NRO, Liber Albus, fol. 67 and *Records of the City of Norwich*, ed. Hudson and Tingey, 1 p. 350.

24 NRO, Liber Albus, fol. 67 and *Records of the City of Norwich*, ed. Hudson and Tingey, 1, p. 351.

25 Tanner, *The Church in Late Medieval Norwich*, p. 150.

26 Maddern, *Violence and Social Order*, pp. 182–3 and 197–8.

27 NRO, Liber Albus, fol. 67 and *Records of the City of Norwich*, ed. Hudson and Tingey, 1, p. 351.

28 *Calendar of Patent Rolls, 1441–6*, p. 199.

29 NRO, Liber Albus fol. 67 and *Records of the City of Norwich*, ed. Hudson and Tingey, 1, p. 351. For the certificate confirming the duration of the imprisonment of Hempsted see NRO, case 9d/4 and Hudson and Tingey, 1, pp. 354–5.

30 *Records of the City of Norwich*, ed. Hudson and Tingey, 1, pp. 351–2 and 343. An exemplification of the restitution of liberties, granted 1 December 1447, is given on pp. 355–6.

31 *Proceedings and Ordinances of the Privy Council*, ed. Nicolas, 5, pp. 229, 235 and 242–4.

32 NRO, Liber Albus, fol. 67ᵛ and *Records of the City of Norwich*, ed. Hudson and Tingey, 1, p. 352–4. This was not the only sealing which took place on this day; an indenture which exempted the Bishop's Palace from the jurisdiction of the city, according to the judgement of the earl of Suffolk, was also sealed on 10 March 1443. See 'Indenture between Thomas Bishop of Norwich and the mayor, sheriffs, and commonalty', ed. Hunter.

33 NRO, Liber Albus, fol. 68 and *Records of the City of Norwich*, ed. Hudson and Tingey, 1, p. 352.

34 Tanner, *The Church in Late Medieval Norwich*, pp. 148 and 148–9.

35 Maddern, *Violence and Social Order*, p. 197.

36 Cheney, *Handbook of Dates*, p. 144.

37 Pettitt, '"Here comes I, Jack Straw"'. Pettitt does mention Gladman's riding, treating it as an example of 'seasonal revelry [which] degenerated into a serious riot' (p. 5). In light of the above discussion it should be clear that this incident is more properly considered as an example of where a festival custom was deployed outside of its calendar context, according to Pettitt's scheme.

38 Cheney, *Handbook of Dates*, p. 144.

39 YCA, House Book 13, fols 121–121^v (my emphasis). See also York *Civic Records 4*, ed. Raine, pp. 28–9, which omits a line from the manuscript.

40 *REED: Lancashire*, ed. George, pp. 11–13 (pp. 11 and 12) (my emphasis).

41 NRO, Liber Albus, fol. 67^v and *Records of the City of Norwich*, ed. Hudson and Tingey, 1, p. 352.

42 NRO, Liber Albus, 67^v and *Records of the City of Norwich*, ed. Hudson and Tingey, 1, p. 351. A further irony was that the mayor and other citizens were taking supper at 'the Kyng's Hedde in Chepe'.

43 Maddern, *Violence and Social Order*, p. 205.

4

Summer games at Coventry in 1480

The city of Coventry is famous for Basil Spence's new cathedral, which rose from the ashes of its medieval forebear, St Michael's. Less well known is that St Michael's had only been a cathedral since 1918, and that the city had another, earlier cathedral, the Benedictine Priory of St Mary's. This first cathedral was closed down in the nationwide suppression of the monasteries by Henry VIII, and had been demolished by the end of the sixteenth century.[1] Like their cousins in medieval Norwich, the citizens of Coventry experienced something of a fraught relationship with their local cathedral priory in the fifteenth century. During the course of a long-running dispute which came to a head in 1480, the citizens of Coventry are alleged to have inflicted grievous damage on the priory's woodlands, by hacking down and carrying off wood from birch, oak and hawthorn trees for use in their summer festivals. The amount of damage alleged was huge: this was not a case of a few twigs or branches that wouldn't be missed, but of one hundred shillings of damage annually. This can be put into perspective when we consider that the parishioners of St Mary at Hill in London paid between 3*d*. and 8*d*. for enough birch-boughs to decorate their entire church at midsummer; working on this basis, the Coventry citizens were carrying off greenery and wood sufficient to fill several hundred parish churches![2] Even if we take into account a measure of exaggeration, and how much wood and greenery might be needed for decorating individual houses and for street bonfires, this is still a considerable amount, and it is no wonder that the priory expressed its outrage at what was happening.

Why did this situation arise in this particular year, 1480? Who was involved? And what did the wholesale deforestation of the priory's woodlands actually achieve? As with the previous chapter, we can bring our new methodology to bear on these questions, considering how this situation came about, and assessing how the meaning of the custom of gathering wood for summer festivals developed in response to wider events in the city. Unsurprisingly, this situation was as much about individuals pursuing their own agendas as it was about antagonisms between the priory and the citizens, or the kind of class war that the safety-valve model presupposes. William Bristow was a local gentleman who had continued his father's acquisitive habits by grazing his animals on lands that belonged to the city, while Laurence Saunders, a dyer, fought valiantly to preserve the rights of the citizens of Coventry against all and sundry, including Bristow, the prior and successive mayors of the city. Saunders's imprisonment for disobedience to the mayor inspired some threatening but also strangely comic poetic warnings that were pinned to church doors in the city, and which invoked Lady Godiva in defence of the citizens's liberties. Saunders also turned out some memorable lines of his own, including his eloquent and no-nonsense resolution that 'Sirs, we shall never have our rights until we have struck off the heads of three or four of the churls who rule us!'[3] Before we consider the main details of the case, we can look briefly at the use of vegetation in festive occasions, and consider how the gathering of wood and foliage for summer festivals falls under our definition of misrule.

In medieval England vegetation and wood were gathered for use on a number of festivals, including holly and ivy for decoration at Christmas, branches for Palm Sunday, rushes and flowers on Easter Day, trees for maypoles at May Day, and wood for bonfires and foliage for decorating houses and churches at midsummer.[4] As regards holly and ivy, Ronald Hutton notes that '[t]he urban churchwardens' accounts for the period virtually all show payments for these evergreens, and their absence from the accounts of country churches is almost certainly due to the fact that they were freely available in the parish'.[5] This would suggest that there was a market for seasonal vegetation in towns, with demand coming from churches, guilds and householders. Individuals wanting vegetation did not necessarily have to pay for it though, since there is also evidence for customary rights to vegetation from private land at festival periods. Although it comes from fourteenth-century France, a well-documented case of vegetation-gathering provides a clear example of the sorts of issues that were at stake when such a practice encroached upon private land. In 1311, a dispute arose between the Hôtel-Dieu of Pontoise and the commune of Chambly, over the use of the wood of the Tour du Lay:

> The wood of the Tour du Lay had been given to the Hôtel-Dieu of Pontoise by Saint Louis in 1261. The religious claimed that they had enjoyed uncontested possession of it since then, but it emerges from the dispute that the inhabitants of Chambly had by custom exercised some rights to gather wood and other materials from it … According to the spokesmen for the religious, in the past the *ministres* of the Hôtel-Dieu, in their goodness and innocence, had allowed the townsfolk to gather flowers and leafy boughs from the wood on feast days during the month of May; but the spokesmen claimed that only twenty persons at a time had gone there for that purpose. On two occasions in early May 1311, however, large crowds from the town – five hundred persons on the first day, more than one thousand on the second – went to the wood at the direction of the communal officials, collecting great quantities of timber and doing extensive damage to the forest.[6]

The full details of the case need not concern us here; for our purposes, it is sufficient to note that in the accord of 1318 that was concluded between the officers of Chambly and the Hôtel-Dieu, the townspeople were limited to collecting just one bundle or handful of greenery each from the wood on 1 May until noon.[7]

Where the gathering of vegetation did encroach upon private land on a particular calendar date or festive period, the practice fits the criteria of misrule, that is, the temporary transgression of a law or norm as part of a festival occasion. In theory taking goods from private land was a very serious offence, and vegetation was no exception to the laws of property. For example, a peace commission for Coventry in February 1397 heard how William and Juliana Wheelwright, Robert Golding and Richard Leygrove had entered a close and carried away trees and shrubs worth 100s. in the previous month. In July of the same year the commission heard how the same William and Juliana, and Richard Tumby had entered the close of Henry Wychard and uprooted and carried away shrubs worth 10 marks in the October of the previous year.[8] Fines for damage to woodland could be steep, from 6s. 8d. for cutting down trees to 10s. for breaking down the hedges and fences around wooded areas.[9] That said, in practice many landowners may have been willing to overlook the appropriation of their foliage at festival times, whether or not it was legal, if the losses were negligible. A further complicating factor was that medieval people also claimed the right to cut firewood, hunt game, play sports and graze their animals on the more marginal 'common' or 'waste' areas of land around towns and villages, and on other fields after harvest was over. These customary rights were gradually being eroded during this period as landowners sought to enclose such lands, hedging and ditching them to provide lucrative grazing pastures for sheep. This restricted people's access to land that had formerly been available for communal use, and unsurprisingly there were many instances where issues of land rights and access became contested.[10]

So in relation to the gathering of wood and foliage for festive occasions, the grounds for misrule were fluid and changing in this period, as relationships between landowners, tenants and local citizens were being redefined. As regards the situation at Coventry in 1480, what appears to have happened is that the customary tolerance of the custom was suspended, due to the sheer scale of the losses involved. The reasons why the damage may have been so large, and what kinds of meaning this gave the custom, will be considered in the course of this chapter.

Disputes with Bristow and the priory, 1480

Coventry's first Leet Book, which covers affairs in the city between 1420 and 1555, is one of the most well-known and widely-cited civic documents from medieval England. It records the discussions and outcomes of the twice-yearly meetings of the 'Leet', which was ostensibly a court, but which had developed as a forum for legislation regulating many aspects of life in the town.[11] Most of the information for the present investigation is drawn from it. Our main interest is in a bill of complaints that was submitted by the prior to the mayor of Coventry in November 1480, and which is copied into the Leet Book. This bill contained a large number of grievances. One such complaint was the rather serious allegation that the terms of the 1355 tripartite indenture, which had settled a land dispute between the priory, the city and Isabella, queen of Edward II, had been broken. It also included the rather embarrassing charge that the townspeople had blocked the gate of the Prior's Orchard with dung, and so prevented him from taking his carriage through it as he was accustomed to do. Other complaints in the bill suggest that activities like the gathering of vegetation during the summer, and the sport of roving (shooting arrows at random targets), were causing great damage to the priory's lands.[12] This is interesting for our purposes as it means that we have a seasonal kind of misrule, the gathering of greenery and branches for summer festivals, caught up in a wider dispute: this is not about the events of one particular day in the year. The prior's bill of complaints was delivered after a turbulent few months in city politics, and it will be helpful to summarise in brief the details of these events and the personalities involved.

Laurence Saunders and William Head, both dyers, were elected as chamberlains of Coventry in January 1480. It was their insistence on fulfilling their duties to the letter rather than according to the customary practices which suited other members of the city government that led to a protracted conflict which ran from April to October of that year.[13] Laurence was the son of William Saunders, a former mayor who had introduced measures to regulate the use of the river Sherbourne and to safeguard the common lands in 1469.[14] After taking up the position of chamberlain in 1480 Laurence spent the next decade and a half campaigning to protect the common lands from encroachment and enclosure, before disappearing into the Fleet prison in November 1495. William Head was a member of the common council, and while he held with Saunders during the events of 1480, he eventually submitted to the rule of the then mayor, William Shore, in October, declaring openly that 'he neuer was of counceill with his felowe'.[15]

There were two disputes which arose during their term of office, and both appear to have resulted from differences of opinion over the responsibilities of the position of chamberlain. One dispute arose with the mayor, William Shore, probably in May 1480. The chamberlains had refused to pay the wages of labourers who had been digging stone for the city wall; 'the seid Laurens there seying presumptuously to the seid maire that they that set them awarke shuld pay for hym'. Head and Saunders were committed to ward and bound under a recognisance of £40 to obey the mayor and council in future; a fine of £4 was also levied.[16] The second dispute arose over rights to pasture on the town's common land, and lasted from April to October 1480. The events of these months are recorded in a petition which the chamberlains submitted to Edward, Prince of Wales, on 20 September; Laurence had requested permission to ride to Southampton, but instead rode to Ludlow to deliver the petition, a copy of which is entered into the Leet Book.[17] The first incident that is described in the petition took place on 8 April of that year, when the chamberlains had seized two hundred sheep belonging to William Deister which were found grazing on the common lands of the city. However, the chamberlains were committed to prison by the mayor for doing so, and the sheep were freed without the fee of 'pynlok' being levied, the charge made by the chamberlains for penning animals which were grazing illegally. Mary Dormer Harris suggests that the animals were seized either because they exceeded the number that each individual was allowed, or because sheep were non-commonable animals.[18] On 18 April, having been prevented from speaking at the Easter Leet, the chamberlains had to pay a bond of £40 each, and were told by the recorder, the city's legal officer, that the charge for penning animals was to be taken as he saw fit. This the chamberlains 'grugged to doo, in so moche as they were solemply sworen to the contrarie. Wheruppon the seid Recordor answered that he wolde rule them be custome and not be sweryng'.[19] Later in the year, when sheep belonging to William Bristow and the prior were grazed on common land, the chamberlains were again preventing from levying a charge.[20] The chamberlains, who were trying to do their job and protect the common lands for the use of all of the citizens, were being overruled in favour of those who had big flocks and the influence to get what they wanted.

After correspondence between the mayor and brethren and the Prince about the chamberlains's petition at the end of September and the beginning of October, a meeting was arranged, and William Head was one of those who rode to Ludlow, after having backed down and agreed to do what he was told.[21] The verdict of the Prince and his advisors, contained in a letter dated 22 October, was that Laurence Saunders was to be punished, and sometime after the receipt of the Prince's reply, Saunders was summoned to appear at St Mary's Hall, where the letter was read to him. 'And theruppon the seid Laurens kneled don before the seid maire and there openly knoleched his offence and dissobeysaunce had and made to the seid maire in tyme past; whereof he besought hym of foryfenes, and there openly and lowely submytted hym self unto the correccion of the seid maire.' Saunders was committed to prison until a bond of the colossal value of £500 was taken from his friends, obliging him to appear at subsequent general sessions 'till certente were had of the sadde demeasnyng of the seid Laurens'.[22]

The prior's bill of complaint was delivered to the mayor and brethren on 16 November, and so it began another dispute just as the episode with the chamberlains was drawing to a close.[23] One of the prior's complaints was that he suffered slander from Laurence Saunders and other persons, who said that he kept pastures exclusively for the priory's own use when they ought to have been available as common; these claims were made in Saunders's petition to the Prince, as we saw above. Other grievances appear to have been of a more personal nature, perhaps as part of a campaign of harassment:

> Also the pepull of the seid citie carryen their donge, ramell [i.e. rubbish] and swepyng of their houses and leyen hit unto the walles and yate of the Priour's Orchard without the Coke Strete Yate, and stoppen up the wey there, that the prior may not have his carriage thorough his orchard as he hath used to have. Where of late tyme they leyde there nothyng but swepyng of their houses, which was carryed a wey by men of the contrey to donge their londe. And nowe be cause they ley there her ramell ther will noman carry a wey there as they were wont to doo, and so hit encreseth dayly more and more to the hyndraunce and grete hurt of the seid priour.[24]

The inclusion of refuse in the deposits meant that people from the country did not now come and take them away, as they had done previously.

The complaints that are most interesting in respect of the present inquiry are those which allege that the people of the city trespassed on and caused damage to priory lands through their sports and festival customs. Most significant for the purpose of this chapter is the fifth article of the bill, in which the prior complained that 'the people of this cite yerely in somer thrown down and beren away the underwode of the seid priour, and birches, holyes, ooke, hawthorn and other at Whitmore Parke and his other closez, and breken his hegges to his hurtes yerely Cs'.[25] As the different types of vegetation named in this article were all used for decorative purposes at summer festivals, the prior's complaint is clear evidence that at Coventry, some of this vegetation was being procured from private lands, without the consent of the landowner. For example, John Stow includes 'greene Birch' as one of the types of vegetation that was used to decorate the doorways of houses in London at the feasts of St John the Baptist and Sts Peter and Paul.[26] In addition, the mention of oak and hawthorn corresponds well with the details of a civic ordinance from Leicester, where in November 1551 it was decreed that any man, woman or child taking oak or hawthorn boughs to set at their doors or windows in summer was to forfeit 12d. and be sent to prison.[27] Other complaints worth noting are the ninth article of the bill, which alleges that people have broken the hedges and dikes of the prior through roving, causing a hundred shillings worth of damage annually and sometimes more, and the eleventh article, which claims that people of the city damaged the Prior's Orchard with shooting and other games. When challenged by the prior's servants, the townsfolk have told them in no uncertain terms that they will have the orchard as their sporting place.[28]

There are two sorts of explanation which we can consider here. It may be that although activities such as vegetation-gathering, roving, shooting and other games were tolerated whilst relations between the town and the priory were amicable, by late 1480 the climate of forbearance had deteriorated to the extent that the prior was no longer willing to sustain them. This view is borne out in some measure by the town's reply, which appeals to the goodwill of lords and gentlefolk, as we shall see below. Another possibility though is that a proportion of the townspeople, dissatisfied with the priory's use of the common lands for grazing sheep, took advantage of these activities in order to cause damage to priory lands, in a situation where other means may not have been possible or to their advantage. Evidence to support this view comes from the fact that the townspeople appear to have been exploiting activities like roving and rubbish disposal to harass the prior; indeed, the prior complained that the obstruction of his orchard was caused by a recent change in the sorts of refuse that the townspeople chose to deposit at its gateway. These are both plausible explanations, and there seems little point in trying to argue for one exclusively against the other, as both factors may have been in play simultaneously. What we can say is that the customarily-tolerated encroachment in question was a negotiated compromise arrived at locally and at a particular historical moment; as such, it was open to change, whether through a shift in attitude on the prior's part or because it was exploited by some of Coventry's inhabitants.

The mayor and brethren took their time in responding to the prior's bill; their answers were recorded on 26 December and delivered to the prior on 2 January 1481.[29] The answers to the complaints about roving and the gathering of vegetation are especially interesting, in that they recognise their transgressive nature but appeal to a customary tolerance of them. In response to the prior's complaints about roving on his land, the mayor and brethren claim that this is a matter concerning individuals rather than the generality, and so, by implication, is not something that they should have to deal with. However, whilst noting that roving is a punishable offence, they go on to appeal to a customary tolerance of the activity; 'such offenders owen to be punysshed be accion atte suyt of the partie greved, for it is grete hurt to all persones havyng lyffelode about the citie, although such rovyng about the citie of London and all other grete cities is suffred'. They also refer to town ordinances forbidding the practice, and suggest that if the names of offenders are given to the mayor, he will seek to reform them.[30]

In response to the prior's complaints about the loss of vegetation, the mayor and brethren make a similar appeal to the principle of customary tolerance:

> To this the seid maire and his brethern seyn that yerely the maistirs of every crafte of the cite be commaundement of the maire chargen the people of their crafte to restreygn such dedes to be don be theym and their servaunts in eschewyng the doughtfull censures of the Chirch and also to be punysshed be the temporell lawe. And yf eny undisposed creature offend to the contrarie ayeynst their will, no defalt therin oweth to be

ascryved in them, remembryng that the people of every gret cite,
as London and other citeez, yerely in somur doon harme to
divers lords and gentyles havyng wods and groves nygh to such
citees be takyng of boughes and treez. And yit the lords and
gentils suffren sych dedes ofte tymes of their goode will, and ofte
tymes the offenders can not be knowen wherthorough
punysshement myght be don.[31]

The mayor and brethren are in effect arguing that by custom,
individuals carrying out certain activities may be regarded as
exempt from the usual legislation. Initially, they claim that the
practice of procuring vegetation is an offence which they
annually denounce. It is the sort of answer that we might expect
to be given by one set of governors to another, invoking the
spiritual and temporal laws for which they each had
responsibility. However, they then go on to excuse such actions
by an expansive appeal to custom. This disjunction in the
statement is striking; it is as if we have two radically different
ways of perceiving the custom of vegetation-gathering, one in
terms of 'the law', where responsibility is taken and delegated,
and the other a much more sober outlook on the realities of
urban life.

It is interesting to note how closely the language of this
passage resembles the defence of Gladman's riding which was
made by the citizens of Norwich *c.* 1450; as we have seen, the
1443 riding was said to be a custom that was practised in any city
or borough throughout the realm on Shrove Tuesday (see
chapter 3). The Coventry example differs, though, in that there
is further evidence to support the claim that the custom was
practised in other cities and indeed in Coventry itself. For
instance an order issued at the Easter Leet in 1448 indicate that
wood was being procured for use at St John's and St Peter's
Eves in this period:

> No one to do damage in pastures, closes, or other places in
> cutting branches, under the penalty of 12s. And that no one
> break the pavement to place branches on it on St John's and St
> Peter's eves.[32]

The mayor and brethren of Coventry cited London as one of the other cities where such practices were tolerated, and the most obvious case to consider in this respect is 'Evil May-Day' in 1517, which has already been mentioned, as has the ordinance from Leicester which forbade the taking of oak or hawthorn boughs. There are clear similarities between this latter passage and the complaint of the prior of Coventry; both specify oak and hawthorn as types of tree that are targeted, and both refer to the summertime. Interestingly enough, this does not appear to have entirely deterred the Leicester townspeople, considering that 'the citizens of Leicester hacked down timber for use on May Day in the woods of Sir Henry Hastings in 1603'.[33] These examples from other towns suggest that the mayor and brethren's appeal to a 'yearly harm that is suffered in every great city' is not to be taken as literal description of a state of affairs which existed in England in this period: other towns including Coventry itself had tried to limit the acquisition of wood and vegetation for summer festivals. Rather, this defence was means of legitimising a local practice under a particular set of circumstances.

In his reply to the mayor and brethren, made 4 January 1481, Prior Deram did not pursue the issue of vegetation-gathering on his land any further.[34] The following Lent, John Boteler, Coventry's steward, went to London to meet the prior and establish a date on which the two parties could meet in Passion Week, but the prior died whilst in London and the matter was postponed. Richard Coventre was elected as the new prior on 4 June 1481, and appears to have been less combative than his predecessor, as no more is heard of the matter.[35]

To sum up, this study has considered how and why the custom of vegetation-gathering became a matter of contention between the priory and the citizens of medieval Coventry in the later fifteenth century, demonstrating that the matter formed only one part of a wider dispute about land use in and around the town in this period. It is not possible to establish with full certainty whether there was a deliberate exploitation of the custom by disaffected citizens to cause excessive damage, or whether a particular prior merely chose to suspend the customary tolerance of this activity at this time. However, the fact that the custom continued to be practised at a time of strained relations at least had the *effect* of producing a sense of harassment, as is evident from the prior's complaints, and this is the more significant conclusion to draw. Clearly, the meaning of the activity changed in response to developing events in the town, and these meanings were also contested at the legal level by means of particular discourses of financial loss (the priory) and of customary tolerance (the mayor and brethren). As regards the outcome of the dispute, it may be inferred that the clandestine activities against the prior had somewhat more success than Laurence Saunders's attempts to pursue his complaints through the proper channels, although the stance of the mayor and brethren in each case appears to have been crucial. We may conclude that misrule became implicated in the local politics of Coventry in such a way as to assume a confrontational meaning, and that when considered as part of a wider situation, significant gains were made by those citizens who undertook such activities.

Notes

1 See Scarisbrick, 'Dissolution of St Mary's'.

2 *The Medieval Records of St. Mary at Hill*, ed. Littlehales, pp. 81, 131, 149 and 163.

3 The vocations and civic offices held by individuals named in this chapter are based upon evidence compiled from the first Leet Book; for more details see Humphrey, 'Dynamics of urban festal culture', chapter 4. See Harris, *Life in an Old English Town*, chapter 12, 'The Lammas lands' for a discussion of the city's disputes with John and William Bristow. For an account of Saunders' campaign see Harris, 'Laurence Saunders, citizen of Coventry': the quotation paraphrases Saunders' words given on p. 646 of this article.

4 Hutton, *Rise and Fall of Merry England*, pp. 5–6, 20–1, 25–6, 27–30 and 37–9.

5 Hutton, *Rise and Fall of Merry England*, p. 5.

6 Lewis, 'Forest rights and the celebration of May', pp. 259–60 (p. 260). I am grateful to John Arnold for this reference.

7 Lewis, 'Forest rights and the celebration of May', p. 266.

8 *Rolls of the Warwickshire and Coventry Sessions of the Peace*, ed. Kimball, pp. 80 and 86.

9 Ault, *Open-Field Farming*, p. 134 and *Statutes of the Realm* 3, p. 980.

10 Hoskins, *Making of the English Landscape*, pp. 117–24.

11 CRO, Leet Book 1. Transcribed and edited as *The Coventry Leet Book*, ed. M. D. Harris, 2 vols, EETS OS 134, 135, 138 and 146 (1907–13). References to the Leet Book in this chapter relate to the original manuscript folios except where stated: the corresponding pages in Harris's edition have not been given, since the folio numbers are easily traceable in the footnotes to that edition.

12 CRO, Leet Book 1, fols 237–238^V and *OED roving* vbl. n. (1) [a].

13 This episode is recorded in CRO, Leet Book 1, fols 234^V–236^V.

14 CRO, Leet Book 1, fols 207–207^V.

15 Head submitted himself to the mayor's rule on October 14 1469 (CRO, Leet Book 1, fol. 235).

16 CRO, Leet Book 1, fol. 234^V.

17 CRO, Leet Book 1, fols 235^V–236.

18 CRO, Leet Book 1, fol. 235^V and *Coventry Leet Book*, ed. Harris, 1, p. 437 n. 2.

19 CRO, Leet Book 1, fol. 235^V.

20 CRO, Leet Book 1, fols 235^V–236.

21 CRO, Leet Book 1, fols 235–235^V.

22 CRO, Leet Book 1, fols 236–236^V (fol. 236^V).

23 The petition is recorded in CRO, Leet Book 1, fols 237–238^V.

24 CRO, Leet Book 1, fol. 237^V.

25 CRO, Leet Book 1, fol. 237.

26 Stow, *Survey of London*, ed. Kingsford, 1, p. 101.

27 *Records of the Borough of Leicester*, ed. Bateson, 3, p. 68.

28 CRO, Leet Book 1, fol. 237.

29 CRO, Leet Book 1, fols 239–241.

30 CRO, Leet Book 1, fol. 239^V.

31 CRO, Leet Book 1, fol. 239.

32 *Coventry Leet Book*, ed. Harris, 1, p. 233 (Harris's translation).

33 Phythian-Adams, 'Ceremony and the citizen', p. 68.

34 CRO, Leet Book 1, fols 242–242^V.

35 CRO, Leet Book 1, fol. 243 and *Calendar of Patent Rolls, 1476–85*, p. 257.

CONCLUSION

This book opened with a quotation from Mikhail Bakhtin, in which he acknowledged that although the 'problem' of carnival in the history of culture is an interesting and complex one, he would not address the subject directly. Rather, as he goes on to say, his interest is in 'the problem of carnivalisation', the influence of carnival forms on literature and literary genre since the Renaissance. We have seen that carnival, or what in the medieval English context is more properly called festive misrule, has continued to fascinate scholars during the 1980s and 1990s. There have been many new studies of the surviving evidence from the Middle Ages, with the result that a great deal more is now known about these lively and topsy-turvy calendar customs. That said, the desire to capture the essence of misrule has tended to polarise opinion into two opposing camps, one that sees misrule as radical and socially oppositional, and other which takes the line that misrule is a safety-valve which dissipates pent-up frustrations and resentments. This situation has made it difficult for those new to the field to get hold of an adequate working definition of misrule, and neither approach has much to say about how to begin studying the evidence for oneself.

In order to overcome this problem the present book has suggested a new approach, which aims to give us both a more credible way of talking about misrule as a form of culture, and a more effective means of investigating its role in the politics and social structure of medieval society. The method presented here gives a practical guide to working with the sources for misrule, and for thinking critically about how they can be interpreted and written up. In addition the case studies have shown how this approach can be applied to two contentious and compelling incidents from the fifteenth century. Of course these are exceptional instances where misrule took place in highly-charged conditions, but their advantage is that they offer plenty of scope for exploring further 'the politics of carnival' of the book's title. The intention is to give students and researchers the confidence to undertake their own analyses, and thereby get beyond the dreary theoretical alternatives that have tended to foreclose any deeper study of the exciting and thought-provoking source material for festive misrule.

As well as offering a new approach to the study of medieval festive drama and popular culture, this book also has implications for a number of other fields of study. The Middle Ages can sometimes seem an isolated area to study and research, and the period is easily caricatured as the mediocre filling between two more significant slices of historical time, the classical period and the modern era. What is interesting about misrule and the wider question of the politics of carnival is that for once it is the medieval form of culture that occupies the central place in this debate. As the literature review in chapter 1 showed, many arguments about the role and vitality of modern popular culture depend for their force upon comparative observations about medieval 'carnival', using Bakhtin's exuberant descriptions as their point of reference. Now, we know that this picture of medieval carnival is hard to reconcile with the evidence: Shrovetide in medieval England was a very different occasion to its continental counterpart, and pointing out this difference is not sheer pedantry, but just a case of getting the basic facts right. That said, trying to convince the modernists of the error of their ways with an erudite paper on the regional variability of horn-lengths in ritual animal disguise is unlikely to get us very far. So we can ask, how can the student of the Middle Ages who believes in the importance of evidence-based research begin to make a real contribution to debates beyond their historical specialism?

Actually the answer is reasonably straightforward, and it involves thinking carefully about the role of a historical perspective in fields like cultural studies and in the humanities more generally. Although the Middle Ages are a popular point of reference in the study of contemporary culture, is this because people are convinced that medieval culture *really is* relevant to an understanding of a late twentieth-century car boot sale? Or is it more the case that Bakhtin said some interesting and exciting things about medieval carnival, and these ideas might help us to understand forms of culture in the present, while also giving a veneer of historical respectability to the analysis? The latter position is closer to expressing what many accounts are doing when they cite Bakhtin, with any reservations about his historical accuracy covered by a feeling that 'even if this isn't the way things really were ... it certainly is the way they ought to have been'.[1] So we can say that while the notion of medieval carnival has been used as a means of generating ideas, precedents and models for the analysis of modern culture, the actual historical 'truth' of the picture has been less important to people than values like inspiration and originality of thought. This is in fact excellent news for a future dialogue between students of medieval festive culture and their modernist counterparts, for as this book has shown, we now have a whole new set of exciting ideas, approaches, case-studies and methodologies to contribute to the debate. The kinds of material that we have covered in this study are at least as interesting as anything that Bakhtin wrote about, not least because we can flesh out in more detail many of the aspects of medieval life which Bakhtin alluded to. More than this, the definitions and approaches outlined in this book have the additional and important virtue of being based upon sound historical research. So we should have the confidence to engage with the contemporary issues and debates which interest us, knowing that our insights are keenly sought and highly regarded outside of the field of early drama studies.

To conclude, the challenge is to move from a position of critique, where we have the role of guardians of knowledge about the Middle Ages, to a position of dialogue, so that the ideas and propositions arising from our research can be brought to bear on questions and issues of wider interest. The most obvious place to begin is in relation to the question of whether popular culture can play a role in social change, since this is where the notion of medieval carnival as a 'safety-valve' has been most heavily used. It is an issue that cannot be resolved merely by making comparisons between cultures five hundred years apart, and instead it needs the kind of close contextual work that has been advocated in this book, and elsewhere.[2] We began this study by looking at how the idea of carnival has enjoyed an important role as a theory of history. It is now time that it took its rightful place in the history of theory, in order that we can move forward with a more progressive approach to the study of popular culture.

Notes

1 DeJean, 'Bakhtin and/in history', p. 226.
2 Davidson, 'Carnival, Lent and drama'; Phythian-Adams, *Local History and Folklore*; Twycross, 'Some approaches to dramatic festivity'; and Humphrey, 'Bakhtin and popular culture'.

BIBLIOGRAPHY

Only short titles are given in the endnotes to each chapter; full references to cited works are given in this bibliography. It is arranged into two sections, primary and secondary sources. The primary sources include state papers, printed and manuscript sources for Coventry and Norwich, and miscellaneous primary sources. The secondary sources include some additional titles which relate to the wider themes of this study.

In the endnotes, if an editor's name is given in the reference, or the reference is to an edition of state papers or to a manuscript, then that publication will be listed under primary sources in this bibliography. All other references will be found in the secondary sources.

Primary sources

Calendar of Patent Rolls, 1441–6.

Calendar of Patent Rolls, 1476–85.

Case 9c/2, Norwich Record Office.

Case 9c/3, Norwich Record Office.

Case 9c/14, Norwich Record Office.

Case 9d/4, Norwich Record Office.

The Coventry Leet Book, ed. M. D. Harris, 2 vols, EETS OS 134, 135, 138 and 146 (1907–13).

'Extract from the books of the Corporation of Norwich', ed. G. Johnson, *Norfolk and Norwich Archaeological Society* 1 (1847), 294–9.

House Book 13, York City Archives.

'Indenture between Thomas Bishop of Norwich and the mayor, sheriffs, and commonalty', in *Ecclesiastical Documents*, ed. J. Hunter, Camden Society (1840), pp. 75–7.

Leet Book 1, Coventry Record Office.

Liber Albus, Norwich Record Office.

The Medieval Records of a London City Church (St. Mary at Hill) A.D. 1420–1559, ed. H. Littlehales, 2 parts, EETS OS 125 and 128 (1904 and 1905).

Proceedings and Ordinances of the Privy Council of England (1386–1542), ed. N. H. Nicolas, 7 vols, 5 (1835).

Records of the Borough of Leicester, ed. M. Bateson, 3 vols, London, 1899–1905.

The Records of the City of Norwich, ed. W. Hudson and J. C. Tingey, 2 vols, Norwich and London, 1906–10.

REED: Lancashire, ed. D. George, Toronto, Buffalo and London, 1991.

Rolls of the Warwickshire and Coventry Sessions of the Peace 1377–1397, ed. E. G. Kimball, Dugdale Society 16 (1939).

Statutes of the Realm, 11 vols (1817), 3.

Stow, J., *A Survey of London*, ed. C. L. Kingsford, 2 vols, Oxford, 1908.

Vergil, P., *The Anglica Historia of Polydore Vergil A.D. 1485–1537*, ed. and trans. D. Hay, Camden Society Third Series 74 (1950).

York Civic Records 4, ed. A. Raine, Yorkshire Archaeological Society Record Series 108 (1943).

Secondary sources

Aers, D. (ed.), *Medieval Literature: Criticism, Ideology and History*, Brighton, 1986.

Aers, D. (ed.), *Culture and History 1350–1600: Essays on English Communities, Identities and Writing*, Hemel Hempstead, 1992.

Anglo, S., 'An early Tudor programme for plays and other demonstrations against the Pope', *Journal of the Warburg and Courtauld Institutes* 20 (1957), 176–9.

Atherton, I., E. Fernie, C. Harper-Bill and H. Smith (eds), *Norwich Cathedral: Church, City and Diocese, 1096–1996*, London and Rio Grande, 1996.

Attreed, L., 'The politics of welcome: ceremonies and constitutional development in later medieval English towns', in Hanawalt and Reyerson (eds), *City and Spectacle in Medieval Europe*, pp. 208–31.

Ault, W. O., *Open-Field Farming in Medieval England: A Study of Village By-Laws*, London and New York, 1972.

Babcock, B. A., 'Introduction', in Babcock (ed.), *The Reversible World*, pp. 13–36.

Babcock, B. A. (ed.), *The Reversible World: Symbolic Inversion in Art and Society*, Ithaca and London, 1978.

Bakhtin, M., *Problems of Dostoevsky's Poetics*, trans. and ed. C. Emerson, Theory and History of Literature 8, Manchester, 1984.

Bakhtin, M., *Rabelais and his World*, trans. H. Iswolsky, Bloomington, 1984.

Barber, C. L., *Shakespeare's Festive Comedy: A Study of Dramatic Form and its Relation to Social Custom*, Princeton, 1959.

Beadle, R. (ed.), *The Cambridge Companion to Medieval English Theatre*, Cambridge, New York and Melbourne, 1994.

Bennett, T., 'A thousand and one troubles: Blackpool Pleasure Beach', in Bennett et al. (eds), *Formations of Pleasure*, pp. 138–55.

Bennett, T., et al. (eds), *Formations of Pleasure*, London, Boston, Melbourne and Henley, 1983.

Bercé, Y.-M., *Fête et révolte: des mentalités populaires du XVIeme au XVIIIeme siécle*, Paris, 1976.

Berrong, R. M., *Rabelais and Bakhtin: Popular Culture in Gargantua and Pantagruel*, Lincoln and London, 1986.

Billington, S., *Mock Kings in Medieval Society and Renaissance Drama*, Oxford, 1991.

Blair, J., and B. Golding (eds), *The Cloister and the World: Essays in Medieval History in Honour of Barbara Harvey*, Oxford, 1996.

Blomefield, F., *An Essay Towards a Topographical History of the County of Norfolk*, 11 vols, 2nd edn, London (1806), 3.

Brandist, C., *Carnival Culture and the Soviet Modernist Novel*, Basingstoke, London and New York, 1996.

Brandist, C. and G. Tihanov (eds), *Materializing Bakhtin: The Bakhtin Circle and Social Theory*, London and New York, 2000.

Bristol, M. D., *Carnival and Theater: Plebian Culture and the Structure of Authority in Renaissance England*, New York, 1985.

Burgess, C., 'Shaping the parish: St Mary at Hill, London, in the fifteenth century', in Blair and Golding (eds), *The Cloister and the World*, pp. 246–86.

Burke, P., *Popular Culture in Early Modern Europe*, revised reprint, Aldershot and Brookfield, 1994.

Butler, J., 'Further reflections on conversations of our time', *diacritics* 27:1 (1997), 13–15.

Camille, M., *Image on the Edge: The Margins of Medieval Art*, London, 1992.

Carroll, L. L., 'Carnival rites as vehicles of protest in Renaissance Venice', *The Sixteenth Century Journal* 16 (1985), 487–502.

Chambers, E. K., *The Mediaeval Stage*, 2 vols, London, 1903.

Cheney, C. R., *Handbook of Dates for Students of English History*, Royal Historical Society Guides and Handbooks 4, London, 1945.

Clark, K. and M. Holquist, *Mikhail Bakhtin*, Cambridge, MA and London, 1984.

Clark, P. and P. Slack (eds), *Crisis and Order in English Towns, 1500–1700: Essays in Urban History*, London, 1972.

Cook, J., 'Carnival and *The Canterbury Tales*', in Aers (ed.), *Medieval Literature*, pp. 169–91.

Cowley, J., *Carnival and Other Seasonal Festivals in the West Indies, U.S.A. and Britain: A Selected Bibliographical Index*, Bibliographies in Ethnic Relations 10, Coventry, 1991.

Cox, J. D. and D. S. Kastan (eds), *A New History of Early English Drama*, New York and Chichester, 1997.

Cressy, D., *Bonfires and Bells: National Memory and the Protestant Calendar in Elizabethan and Stuart England*, London, 1989.

Davidson, C., 'Carnival, Lent, and early English drama', *Research Opportunities in Renaissance Drama* 36 (1997), 123–42.

Davis, N. M., 'The playing of miracles in England between *c.*1350 and the Reformation', unpublished Ph.D. thesis, University of Cambridge, 1977.

Davis, N. Z., 'The reasons of misrule: youth groups and charivaris in sixteenth-century France', *Past and Present* 50 (1971), 41–75.

Davis, N. Z., *Society and Culture in Early Modern France*, London, 1975.

Davis, N. Z., 'Women on top: symbolic sexual inversion and political disorder in early modern Europe', in Babcock (ed.), *The Reversible World*, pp. 147–90.

DeJean, 'Bakhtin and/in history', in Stolz, Titunik and Doležel (eds), *Language and Literary Theory*, pp. 225–40.

Demidowicz, G. (ed.), *Coventry's First Cathedral: The Cathedral and Priory of St Mary*, Paul Watkins Medieval Studies 17, Stamford, 1994.

Dentith, S., *Bakhtinian Thought: An Introductory Reader*, London, 1995.

Dibben, A. A., 'Midland archives collections: II. The City Record Office, Coventry', *Midland History* 2 (1973–4), 99–109.

Dollimore, J., *Sexual Dissidence: Augustine to Wilde, Freud to Foucault*, Oxford, 1991.

Dollimore, J. and A. Sinfield (eds), *Political Shakespeare: Essays in Cultural Materialism*, 2nd edn, Manchester, 1994.

Dorson, R. M., *The British Folklorists: A History*, London, 1968.

Douglas, M., *Purity and Danger: An Analysis of Concepts of Pollution and Taboo*, London, 1966.

Duffy, E., *The Stripping of the Altars: Traditional Religion in England c.1400–c.1580*, New Haven and London, 1992.

Dyer, C., 'The Rising of 1381 in Suffolk: its origins and participants', *Proceedings of the Suffolk Institute of Archaeology and History* 36 (1988), 274–87.

Eagleton, T., *Walter Benjamin, or, Towards a Revolutionary Criticism*, London, 1981.

Eco, U., 'The frames of comic "freedom"', in Sebeok (ed.), *Carnival!*, pp. 1–9.

Evans, R., 'Body politics: engendering medieval cycle drama', in Evans and Johnson (eds), *Feminist Readings in Middle English Literature*, pp. 112–39.

Evans, R. and L. Johnson (eds), *Feminist Readings in Middle English Literature: The Wife of Bath and All Her Sect*, London and New York, 1994.

Farrell, T. J. (ed.), *Bakhtin and Medieval Voices*, Gainsville, 1996.

Flaherty, P., 'Reading carnival: towards a semiotics of history', *Clio* 15 (1986), 411–28.

Foucault, M., *Language, Counter-Memory, Practice: Selected Essays and*

Interviews, trans. D. F. Bouchard and S. Simon, ed. D. F. Bouchard, Ithaca and New York, 1977.

Foucault, M., 'A preface to transgression', in Bouchard (ed.), *Language, Counter-Memory, Practice*, pp. 29–52.

Gash, A., 'Carnival against Lent: the ambivalence of medieval drama', in Aers (ed.), *Medieval Literature*, pp. 74–98.

Gluckman, M., *Order and Rebellion in Tribal Africa: Collected Essays*, New York, 1963.

Goldberg, P. J. P., *Women, Work and Life Cycle in a Medieval Economy: Women in York and Yorkshire c.1300–1520*, Oxford, 1992.

Greenfield, P. H., 'Festive drama at Christmas in aristocratic households', in Twycross (ed.), *Festive Drama,* pp. 34–40.

Gregson, N. and L. Crewe, 'The bargain, the knowledge, and the spectacle: making sense of consumption in the space of the car-boot sale', *Environment and Planning D: Society and Space* 15 (1997), 87–112.

Griffiths, R. A., *The Reign of King Henry VI: The Exercise of Royal Authority, 1422–1461*, London, 1981.

Grössinger, C., *The World Upside-Down: English Misericords*, London, 1997.

Gurevich, A., *Medieval Popular Culture: Problems of Belief and Perception*, trans. J. M. Bak and P. A. Hollingsworth, Cambridge Studies in Oral and Literate Culture 14, Cambridge, 1988.

Gurevich, A., '"High and low": the medieval grotesque', in Gurevich, *Medieval Popular Culture*, pp. 176–210.

Hall, J., 'Falstaff, Sancho Panza and Azdak: carnival and history', *Comparative Criticism* 7 (1985), 127–45.

Hamburger, J. F., review of Camille, *Image on the Edge*, in *The Art Bulletin* 75 (1993), 319–27.

Hanawalt, B. A., *Growing Up in Medieval London: The Experience of Childhood in History*, Oxford, 1993.

Hanawalt, B. A. and K. L. Reyerson (eds), *City and Spectacle in Medieval Europe*, Medieval Studies at Minnesota 6, London and Minneapolis, 1994.

Happé, P., 'A guide to criticism of medieval English theatre', in Beadle (ed.), *The Cambridge Companion to Medieval English Theatre*, pp. 312–43.

Happé, P., *English Drama before Shakespeare*, London and New York, 1999.

Harper, J., *The Forms and Orders of Western Liturgy from the Tenth to the Eighteenth Century: A Historical Introduction and Guide for Students and Musicians*, Oxford, 1991.

Harris, M., *Festivals of Aztecs, Moors, and Christians: Dramatizations of Reconquest in Spain and Mexico*, Austin, 2000.

Harris, M. D., 'Laurence Saunders, citizen of Coventry', *English Historical Review* 9 (1894), 633–51.

Harris, M. D., *Life in an Old English Town: A History of Coventry from the Earliest Times Compiled from Official Records*, London, 1898.

Hilton, R. H., *English and French Towns in a Feudal Society*, Cambridge, 1992.

Hindley, A. (ed.), *Drama and Community: People and Plays in Medieval Europe*, Medieval Texts and Cultures of Northern Europe 1, Turnhout, 1999.

Hirschkop, K. and D. Shepherd (eds), *Bakhtin and Cultural Theory*, Manchester and New York, 1989.

Horner, O., 'Christmas at the Inns of Court', in Twycross (ed.), *Festive Drama*, pp. 41–53.

Hoskins, W. G., *The Making of the English Landscape*, with introduction and commentary by C. Taylor, London, Sydney, Auckland and Toronto, 1988.

Humphrey, C., '"To make a new king": seasonal drama and local politics in Norwich, 1443', *Medieval English Theatre* 17 (1995), 29–41.

Humphrey, C., 'The dynamics of urban festal culture in later medieval England', unpublished D.Phil. thesis, University of York, 1997.

Humphrey, C., 'Festive drama and community politics in late medieval Coventry', in Hindley (ed.), *Drama and Community*, pp. 217–30.

Humphrey, C., 'Bakhtin and the study of popular culture: re-thinking carnival as a historical and analytical concept', in Brandist and Tihanov (eds), *Materializing Bakhtin*, pp. 164–72.

Humphrey, C., 'The world upside down in theory and as practice: a new approach to the study of medieval misrule', *Medieval English Theatre* 21 (1999), 5–20.

Hutton, R., *The Rise and Fall of Merry England: The Ritual Year 1400–1700*, Oxford and New York, 1994.

Hutton, R., *The Stations of the Sun: A History of the Ritual Year in Britain*, Oxford and New York, 1996.

James, E. O., *Seasonal Feasts and Festivals*, London, 1961.

James, M., 'Ritual, drama and social body in the late medieval English town', *Past and Present* 98 (1983), 3–29.

Jeffery, P., *The Parish Church of St. Mary-at-Hill in the City of London*, London, 1996.

Johnston, A. F., 'The continental connection: a reconsideration', in Knight (ed), *The Stage as Mirror*, pp. 7–24.

Justice, S., *Writing and Rebellion: England in 1381*, The New Historicism: Studies in Cultural Poetics 27, Berkeley and London, 1994.

Kastan, D. S. and P. Stallybrass (eds), *Staging the Renaissance: Reinterpretations of Elizabethan and Jacobean Drama*, London, 1991.

Kastan, D. S. and P. Stallybrass, 'Introduction: staging the Renaissance', in Kastan and Stallybrass (eds), *Staging the Renaissance*, pp. 1–14.

Klaniczay, G., *The Uses of Supernatural Power: The Transformation of Popular Religion in Medieval and Early-Modern Europe*, trans. S. Singerman and ed. K. Margolis, Cambridge, 1990.

Klaniczay, G., 'The carnival spirit: Bakhtin's theory on the culture of popular laughter', in Klaniczay, *The Uses of Supernatural Power*, pp. 10–27.

Knight, A. E. (ed.), *The Stage as Mirror: Civic Theatre in Late Medieval Europe*, Cambridge, 1997.

Kohl, P. R., 'Looking through a glass onion: rock and roll as a modern manifestation of carnival', *Journal of Popular Culture* 27 (1993), 143–61.

LaCapra, D., *Rethinking Intellectual History: Texts, Contexts, Language*, London and Ithaca, 1983.

Lancashire, I., *Dramatic Texts and Records of Britain: A Chronological Topography to 1558*, Studies in Early English Drama 1, Toronto and Buffalo, 1984.

Laroque, F., *Shakespeare's Festive World: Elizabethan Seasonal Entertainment and the Professional Stage*, trans. J. Lloyd, Cambridge, 1991.

Le Roy Ladurie, E., *Carnival: A People's Uprising at Romans, 1579–80*, trans. M. Feeney, London, 1980.

Leach, E. R. (ed.), *Dialectic in Practical Religion*, Cambridge, 1968.

Leinwand, T. B., 'Negotiation and New Historicism', *Publications of the Modern Language Association of America* 105 (1990), 477–90.

Levine, L. W., *Black Culture and Black Consciousness: Afro-American Folk Thought from Slavery to Freedom*, New York, 1977.

Lewis, A. W., 'Forest rights and the celebration of May: two documents from the French Vexin, 1311–1318', *Mediaeval Studies* 53 (1991), 259–77.

Lilley, K. D., *Modernizing the Medieval City: Urban Design and Civic Improvement in the Middle Ages*, Royal Holloway Department of Geography Research Papers, 1999.

Lindenbaum, S., 'The Smithfield tournament of 1390', *Journal of Medieval and Renaissance Studies* 20 (1990), 1–20.

Lindenbaum, S., 'Ceremony and oligarchy: the London Midsummer Watch', in Hanawalt and Reyerson (eds), *City and Spectacle in Medieval Europe*, pp. 171–88.

Lindenbaum, S., 'Rituals of exclusion: feasts and plays of the English religious fraternities', in Twycross (ed.), *Festive Drama*, pp. 54–65.

Mackenzie, N., 'Boy into bishop: a festive role-reversal', *History Today* 37, (December 1987), 10–16.

MacLean, S.-B., 'Hocktide: a reassessment of a popular pre-Reformation festival', in Twycross (ed.), *Festive Drama*, pp. 233–41.

Maddern, P. C., *Violence and Social Order: East Anglia 1422–1442*, Oxford, 1992.

Manning, R. B., *Hunters and Poachers: A Social and Cultural History of Unlawful Hunting in England, 1485–1640*, Oxford, 1993.

Mansfield, M. C., *The Humiliation of Sinners: Public Penance in Thirteenth-Century France*, Ithaca and London, 1995.

McRee, B. R., 'Religious gilds and civic order: the case of Norwich in the late Middle Ages', *Speculum* 67 (1992), 69–97.

McRee, B. R., 'Peacemaking and its limits in late medieval Norwich', *English Historical Review* 109 (1994), 831–66.

Mellinkoff, R., 'Riding backwards: theme of humiliation and symbol of evil', *Viator* 4 (1973), 153–76.

Muir, E., *Mad Blood Stirring: Vendetta in Renaissance Italy*, Baltimore and London, 1998.

Norbeck, E., 'African rituals of conflict', *American Anthropologist* 65 (1963), 1254–79.

Patterson, L., 'On the margin: postmodernism, ironic history, and medieval studies', *Speculum* 65 (1990), 87–108.

Pettitt, T., '"Here comes I, Jack Straw": English folk drama and social revolt', *Folklore* 95 (1984), 3–20.

Pettitt, T., 'Protesting inversions: charivary as folk pageantry and folk-law', *Medieval English Theatre* 21 (1999).

Phythian-Adams, C., 'Ceremony and the citizen: the communal year at Coventry 1450–1550', in Clark and Slack (eds), *Crisis and Order in English Towns*, pp. 57–85.

Phythian-Adams, C., *Local History and Folklore: A New Framework*, London, 1975.

Phythian-Adams, C., *Desolation of a City: Coventry and the Urban Crisis of the Late Middle Ages*, Cambridge, 1979.

Phythian-Adams, C., 'Ceremony and the citizen: the communal year at Coventry 1450–1550', in Rosser and Holt (eds), *The Medieval Town*, pp. 238–64.

Poole, B., *Coventry: Its History and Antiquities*, London and Coventry, 1870.

Randall, L. M. C., *Images in the Margins of Gothic Manuscripts*, Berkeley and Los Angeles, 1966.

Rappaport, S., *Worlds Within Worlds: Structures of Life in Sixteenth-Century London*, Cambridge Studies in Population, Economy and Society in Past Time 7, Cambridge, 1989.

Rigby, P., 'Some Gogo rituals of "purification": an essay on social and moral categories', in Leach (ed.), *Dialectic in Practical Religion*, pp. 153–78.

Rosser, G. and R. Holt (eds), *The Medieval Town: A Reader in English Urban History 1200–1540*, London, 1990.

Rubin, M., *Corpus Christi: The Eucharist in Late Medieval Culture*, Cambridge, 1991.

Sacks, D. H., *The Widening Gate: Bristol and the Atlantic Economy, 1450–1700*, The New Historicism: Studies in Cultural Poetics 15, Berkeley, Los

Angeles and London, 1991.

Scarisbrick, J. J., 'The dissolution of St Mary's Priory, Coventry', in Demidowicz (ed.), *Coventry's First Cathedral*, pp. 158–68.

Schechner, R., *Between Theater and Anthropology*, Philadelphia, 1985.

Schechner, R., *Performance Theory*, revised edition, New York and London, 1988.

Scott, J. C., *Domination and the Arts of Resistance: Hidden Transcripts*, New Haven and London, 1990.

Sebeok, T. A. (ed.), *Carnival!*, Approaches to Semiotics 64, Berlin, 1984.

Shahar, S., 'The boy bishop's feast: a case-study in church attitudes towards children in the high and late Middle Ages', *Studies in Church History* 31 (1994), 243–60.

Sharp, T., *A Dissertation on the Pageants or Dramatic Mysteries Anciently Performed at Coventry*, [Coventry, 1825], repr. East Ardsley, 1973.

Simon, E., 'Organizing and staging carnival plays in late medieval Lübeck: a new look at the archival record', *Journal of English and Germanic Philology* 92 (1993), 57–72.

Sinfield, A., *Faultlines: Cultural Materialism and the Politics of Dissident Reading*, Oxford, 1992.

Somerset, A., 'New Historicism: old history writ large? Carnival, festivity and popular culture in the West Midlands', *Medieval and Renaissance Drama in England* 5 (1991), 245–55.

Sponsler, C., 'Writing the unwritten: morris dance and the study of medieval theatre', *Theatre Survey* 38 (1997), 73–95.

Stallybrass, P. and A. White, *The Politics and Poetics of Transgression*, London, 1986.

Stolz, B. A., I. R. Titunik and L. Doležel (eds), *Language and Literary Theory*, Papers in Slavic Philology 5, Michigan, 1984.

Storey, R. L., *The End of the House of Lancaster*, London, 1966.

Strutt, J., *The Sports and Pastimes of the People of England*, new edition, London, 1838.

Tanner, N. P., *The Church in Late Medieval Norwich, 1370–1532*, Studies and Texts 66, Toronto, 1984.

Thompson, A. H., *The History of the Hospital and the New College of the Annunciation of St. Mary in the Newarke, Leicester*, Leicester, 1937.

Turner, V. W., *The Ritual Process: Structure and Anti-Structure*, London, 1969.

Twycross, M. (ed.), *Festive Drama: Papers from the Sixth Triennial Colloquium of the International Society for the Study of Medieval Theatre*, Cambridge, 1996.

Twycross, M., 'Some approaches to dramatic festivity, especially processions', in Twycross (ed.), *Festive Drama*, pp. 1–33.

White, P. W., 'Politics, topical meaning, and English theater audiences 1485–1575', *Research Opportunities in Renaissance Drama* 34 (1995), 41–54.

Womack, P., 'Imagining communities: theatres and the English nation in the sixteenth century', in Aers (ed.), *Culture and History 1350–1600*, pp. 91–145.

Yeo, E. and S. Yeo (eds), *Popular Culture and Class Conflict 1590–1914: Explorations in the History of Labour and Leisure*, Brighton, 1981.

Yeo, E. and S. Yeo, 'Ways of seeing: control and leisure versus class and struggle', in Yeo and Yeo (eds), *Popular Culture and Class Conflict*, pp. 128–54.

INDEX